ONE FOR SORROW...

A NOTE ON THE ILLUSTRATIONS

The decorations in this book are by Thomas Bewick – though a few may be by his pupils – the leading English wood engraver of his day, who was born near Newcastle upon Tyne, Northumberland, in 1753. A naturalist, sportsman and ornithologist as well as an artist, his published works include *A General History of Quadrupeds*, the two-volume *A History of British Birds*, several editions of Æsop's *Fables* and *A Memoir of Thomas Bewick written by himself*, which was published in 1862, thirty-four years after his death. Pre-eminent among wood engravers in his own time – he was praised by, among others, Wordsworth and Charlotte Brontë – he remains one of the greatest of illustrators.

ONE FOR SORROW...

A BOOK OF OLD-FASHIONED LORE

CHLOE RHODES

Michael O'Mara Books Limited

This paperback edition first published in 2016

First published in Great Britain in 2011 by
Michael O'Mara Books Limited
9 Lion Yard
Tremadoc Road
London SW4 7NQ

A CIP catalogue record for this book is available from the British Library.

Papers used by Michael O'Mara Books Limited are natural, recyclable products made from wood grown in sustainable forests. The manufacturing processes conform to the environmental regulations of the country of origin.

ISBN: 978-1-78243-518-1 in paperback print format
ISBN: 978-1-84317-779-1 in EPub format
ISBN: 978-1-84317-780-7 in Mobipocket format

1 2 3 4 5 6 7 8 9 10

Cover design by BoldandNoble.com
Designed and typeset by Ana Bježančević

Printed and bound by CPI Group (UK) Ltd, Croydon, CR0 4YY

www.mombooks.com

CONTENTS

For Lorna Rhodes, my Grandma, and for
Iris Dyson, my great-godmother.

INTRODUCTION

We live in an age of scientific and technological enlightenment. We understand the electromagnetic and gravitational forces that exert their influence on our planet; we've sent satellites into space that allow us to forecast the weather, navigate the seas and communicate face to digitized face with friends on the opposite side of the earth. We know how diseases spread, both through populations and within the body, and in most cases, we know how to cure them. We've identified the sections of the brain responsible for making us feel happy, motivated, ashamed; we even know the chemical responses that occur when we fall in love. We've cloned sheep, genetically modified corn, created new human life in a Petri dish and calculated the rate at which the universe is expanding into infinity. And yet, what shapes the discourse of our daily lives is not modern insight but ancient wisdom.

Sayings from folklore that have been passed from one generation to the next, often without adaptation despite centuries of change, are still a key facet of our conversations. Many have a pleasing rhythm or rhyme that lend a certain musicality to our speech and they are usually passed on within families by word of mouth. It has, however, been customary for lovers of language to catalogue these sayings every century or so and preserve them in writing. One such collector of proverbs was the eighteenth-century physician Thomas Fuller, who compiled a volume called *Gnomologia: Adagies and Proverbs, Wise Sentences and Witty Sayings*, which was published in London in 1732. In the preface he explains: 'Because verses are easier got by heart, and stick faster in the memory than prose; and because ordinary people use to be much taken with the clinking of syllables; many of our proverbs are so formed . . . This little artifice, I imagine, was contrived purposely to make the sense abide the longer in the memory, by reason of its oddness and archness.'

It certainly worked as a way of lodging these sayings in our collective consciousness, but sometimes the oddness and archness Fuller describes means that we use these phrases instinctively, knowing how to use them without really knowing where they come from or what they actually mean. This book attempts to unravel the secrets of these phrases' origins and the contexts within which they might first have been used. For the most part, they can be divided into three categories: the moral, the practical and the superstitious.

Grouped together, the proverbs in the moral bracket create a kind of guidebook on how to be good and tend to have their origins in country customs, parables from the Bible, Æsop's *Fables* and the musings of Ancient Greek philosophers. We use them today to remind others, and sometimes ourselves, of the perils of vices like the greed of the farmer who killed the goose that laid the golden egg and the merits of virtues such as the graciousness displayed by those who don't look a gift horse in the mouth. They also served as a way of helping people understand human behaviour (birds of a feather flock together) and the trials of life (there's no rose without a thorn).

Those sayings that have some practical application are most often rooted in observations of the natural world, and in the days before modern technology were used to predict the weather. In medieval England, when many of these sayings were first used, the patterns of rainfall and sunshine were a matter of life and death. The weather determined the fertility of the earth and, as the devastating famines of the early Middle Ages had demonstrated, the survival of the populace depended on the success of each year's harvest. A warm, dry summer would ensure that crops ripened, that there was enough hay to feed the livestock and that the harvest could take place at the optimum time, so farmers turned to the trees and noted that 'Ash before Oak the summer is all a soak, Oak before Ash the summer is but a splash.' A warm winter on the other hand could cause crops to begin growing too early only to be killed off when the frosts arrived, which is why 'a snow year is a rich year.' Many of the phrases from weather lore that we use as a kind of rustic commentary on the weather today were once the only means people had of planning and preparing for their own survival.

The sayings that stem from superstition are perhaps those that on the surface seem least applicable today. The secularization of Western society has diluted the blend of religious zeal and belief in the supernatural that lay behind them, but they have become so well woven into the fabric of our lives that we count magpies and make wishes on ladybirds without pausing to think about why we're doing it. And the Devil, who in the God-fearing days of our ancestors was held responsible for all manner of ills, still makes regular appearances in our vocabulary, in obvious ways in phrases like 'talk of the Devil', and more covertly in sayings like 'needs must . . . (when the Devil drives)'.

Perhaps part of the reason these phrases from folklore endure is our yearning for a simpler age. There's comfort to be had from knowing that the human condition hasn't been altered by the advancement in our understanding of the world. But maybe it's also because of the immediacy with which they relate to our own experiences of life. While we could quite easily switch on the television to watch the weather forecast, it is still deeply satisfying to see a red sky at night and anticipate the clear skies that would have delighted the shepherds of the Middle Ages. It still feels relevant, despite the years that have passed since traditional forges closed, to strike while the iron's hot and, for all our understanding of human psychology, it is still a comfort in the depths of despair to be told that the darkest hour is that before the dawn.

Over centuries, if not millennia, words of wisdom have been passed down, first by word of mouth and then included in poetry, plays, histories and, of course, collections of adages, maxims, aphorisms, homilies and gnomes (not the garden variety). Just as there are many terms for them, there are many versions, as they have been altered to suit their context. Some become distrustful when burnt, some when bitten; where magpies are few, they have been replaced by crows; at sea and in harbours it is the sailor or the fisherman who is delighted by red skies. The meaning, however, generally remains the same. So do not be disappointed or feel cheated if you find the sayings in forms that differ from those you knew. The ones included in this book are not necessarily the 'correct' versions – they are just the versions that first came to me. To include every variant would make a very long and over-earnest book.

As Thomas Fuller said of his collection, this is my effort to 'throw together a vast confused heap of unsorted things old and new which you may pick over and make use of according to your judgement and pleasure.'

ONE FOR SORROW, TWO FOR JOY

One for sorrow
Two for joy
Three for a girl
Four for a boy
Five for silver
Six for gold
Seven for a secret never to be told.

This well-known rhyme has been around since the mid-nineteenth century when the number of magpies seen foraging together was regarded as forecaster of future events. Interestingly, everybody knows what bird is meant (usually the magpie, but in some parts of the world where magpies are rarely if ever seen, crows or other corvids) – though no kind of bird at all is mentioned in the rhyme.

As with many proverbs passed down in the oral tradition there are numerous regional variations; in Ireland and the US the most commonly recited version goes:

One for sorrow
Two for mirth

Three for a funeral
Four for a birth
Five for heaven
Six for hell
Seven's the Devil his own self.

In Manchester the rhyme has additional lines: 'Eight for a wish, Nine for a kiss, Ten for a surprise you should be careful not to miss, Eleven for health, Twelve for wealth, Thirteen beware it's the devil himself.'

Common to all the versions is the notion that a lone magpie is a harbinger of sorrow and therefore unlucky. The bird's bad reputation may stem from its behaviour; it is known for stealing shiny objects and for killing other birds' chicks to feed its own, but it seems more likely that the superstitions that surround it have their roots in folklore. British legend has it that the magpie was the only bird not to sing to comfort Jesus as he suffered on the cross, while in Scotland the bird was believed to hold a drop of the Devil's blood under its tongue. If you do see a solitary magpie though you can ward off bad luck by saluting, spitting over your shoulder three times, doffing your hat or saying, 'Morning, Mr Magpie, how are you this fine day?' Alternatively, you could say 'Good morning, Mr Magpie, how's your wife?' (in the hope that the bird's mate is hiding somewhere near by to turn your sorrow into joy).

Somewhat sounder is the proverb 'A single magpie in spring foul weather will bring', from the birds' habit of feeding together only in fine weather.

BIRDS OF A FEATHER FLOCK TOGETHER

This sixteenth-century proverb first appeared in a 1599 dictionary compiled by the English lexicographer and linguist John Minsheu. It is thought to have been in use for at least fifty years by the time it made it into print and a slightly different version of the phrase can be found in the naturalist, physician and nonconformist churchman William Turner's *The Rescuynge of the Romishe Fox*, published in 1545:

> *Byrdes of on kynde and color flok and flye allwayes together.*

Like many sayings from folklore it comes from observation of the natural world. Birds of the same species will often form a flock, flying in the same direction instinctively to avoid being singled out by a bird of prey. The phrase is used to imply that people will gravitate towards others who share their tastes or beliefs. By the seventeenth century it was being used in reference to the influence of bad behaviour; in William Secker's handbook for Christian living *The Consistent Christian*, published in 1660, he quotes the proverb and explains: 'To be too *intimate* with sinners – is to *intimate* that you are a sinner.' These days it's sometimes used with a knowing wink to suggest that someone who associates with criminals is likely to be one themselves, though it applies equally to friends or couples who are well matched because they have views or characteristics in common.

RED SKY AT NIGHT

Red sky at night, shepherd's delight
Red sky in the morning, shepherd's
warning.

This ancient proverb is one of our best-known weather-lore rhymes and dates back to at least the fourteenth century. The earliest known printed example of the saying appears in Middle English in John Wycliffe's Bible, published in 1395, and by the time the Authorized King

James version was produced in 1611 it contained what was recognizably an early incarnation of today's version:

When it is evening, ye say, It will be fair weather: for the sky is red. And in the morning, It will be foul weather to day: for the sky is red and lowring. (Matthew 16:2-3)

Shepherds, along with sailors (who appear in an alternative version of the rhyme) had to find ways of predicting the weather in order to plan the best course of action for the day ahead. Sheep might need to be brought down from the hills if heavy rain threatened and, in the days before meteorological technology, those whose livelihoods depended on the weather developed their own forecasting methods. This one happens to be fairly accurate; redness is seen in the sky opposite the sun when light rays hit water droplets in the atmosphere. In the northern hemisphere where the sun rises in the east and sets in the west and weather systems move from west to east, red sky at night means that clouds are moving away from us, while red sky in the morning means that water-laden air is heading our way.

ONE SWALLOW DOESN'T MAKE A SUMMER

This is a translation of one of the many ancient Greek proverbs gathered and recorded by the Dutch humanist Erasmus in the early sixteenth century. It first appears in English in Richard Taverner's transcription of the Latin proverbs of Erasmus, *Prouerbes or adagies with newe addicions, gathered out of the Chiliades of Erasmus*, in 1539:

It is not one swalowe that bryngeth in somer. It is not one good qualitie that maketh a man good.

This early version refers to the fact that in Europe and America the swallow is a summer visitor, arriving to breed in May and staying until September. The original Greek proverb suggests that nothing should be judged on the basis of just one facet of the whole, though the saying was popularized and its meaning subtly altered by its appearance in Æsop's *Fables*, the first English version of which was published by William Caxton in 1484. The fable 'The Spendthrift and the Swallow' tells the story of a young man who has frittered away all his money and has only the clothes he stands up in. Then he sees a swallow on a bright spring day and thinking summer has come, sells his coat as well. But a hard frost comes, the swallow dies and the young man almost perishes with cold. Æsop's moral tale has found its way into modern parlance as a warning that we shouldn't assume success is on the way on the strength of one achievement.

AFTER A STORM COMES A CALM

This is an example of the kind of country saying that brought comfort by applying the laws of the natural world to the trials of human life. It is first recorded in William Langland's allegorical poem *Piers Plowman*, written during the years 1360–87: 'After sharpest shoures . . . moste shene is the sonne.' Its literal meaning, that stormy weather is usually followed by bright, clear skies, came from observations of weather patterns and formed an important part of fourteenth-century weather lore.

Though the farmers and sailors who used the saying can have understood little of the science behind it, what they witnessed was rising air during a storm, which causes high winds and rain, followed by a period of clearer skies and stillness caused by descending air after the storm.

A similar pattern can be observed in human emotion and by the sixteenth century the saying had also become a way of consoling someone in their grief, or reassuring people suffering hardship that more serene times would soon come.

In modern usage there is often an implication that tranquillity can only be achieved after a period of intense activity and stress, or that people who have had turbulent times in their personal lives are more likely to appreciate the calmness brought by a more sedate existence afterwards.

We also use the phrase 'the calm before the storm', which comes from the eerie stillness that can precede a hurricane or cyclone, to describe the strange peace that comes before upheaval.

MARCH COMES IN LIKE A LION AND GOES OUT LIKE A LAMB

This early seventeenth-century saying refers to the fact that in northern Europe and North America, March usually begins with storms and ends with calm weather. There are some who assert that the saying has its roots in astrology and relates to the relative positions of constellations at the beginning and end of the month: Leo, the Lion rising on the eastern horizon and Aries, the Ram (sometimes lamb) sinking on the western horizon. This seems more likely just happy coincidence – the ferocious storms that often herald the arrival of March and the calm, mild days that accompany its end are more regularly cited as its source.

The earliest known appearance of the phrase in print is a playful one. English playwright John Fletcher wrote in his 1625 tragicomedy *A Wife for a Month*: "'I would chuse March, for I would come in like a Lion.' 'But you'd go out like a Lamb when you went to hanging.'" And in the writer and historian James Howell's historical allegory *Dodona's Grove* (1640): 'Like the moneth of March, which entreth like a Lion, but goeth out like a Lamb.'

In colonial America the phrase appeared in both Ames's *Almanack* of 1740, and plantation owner and author William Byrd's *Another Secret Diary* for the same year. By 1788, when America's second president John Adams recorded it in his own diary, it was a well established enough piece of folklore for him to refer to it as a 'farmer's proverb.'

BETTER A WOLF IN THE FOLD, THAN A FINE FEBRUARY

This ancient phrase might sound strange to modern ears, but our preference for mild winters would have been anathema to our farming forebears whose livelihoods were threatened by too much warmth early in the year. Fine weather in February can cause plants and crops to begin their spring-time growth prematurely, which puts them at risk of being damaged if more seasonal cold weather returns and brings a hard frost. (See also 'If February gives much snow,' p. 180.)

For early farmers, the protection of their livestock and crops was crucial to their survival and this phrase compares the two biggest disasters that might befall them. A wolf in the flock would mean the loss of several sheep but too mild a winter would ruin a farmer's entire harvest. It has its roots in Virgil's pastoral poems, the *Eclogues*, thought to have been written between 42 and 38 BC, in which wolves appear regularly as a cunning and ruthless enemy of man. The poems tell the stories of the lives and loves of rural herdsmen and feature a shepherdess named Amaryllis. In Eclogue III: 'Menalcas, Damoetas, Palaemon,' Virgil writes:

Fell as the wolf is to the folded flock,
Rain to ripe corn, Sirocco to the trees,
The wrath of Amaryllis is to me.

'A wolf in the fold' is also now widely used as a stand-alone phrase when someone fears there is an enemy in their midst.

DOG DAYS BRIGHT AND CLEAR

Dog Days bright and clear
indicate a happy year.
But when accompanied by rain, for
better times our hopes are vain.

The Old Farmer's Almanack, which has been published in the United States since 1792, describes the dog days as the forty days beginning, in the northern hemisphere, on 3 July and ending 11 August . (The dates vary according to latitude and climate.) They were named 'dog days' by the ancient Greeks after the dog star Sirius, the brightest in the constellation Canis Major (Big Dog), and coincided with the days on which Sirius rose with the sun. The Greeks and Romans believed that the hot, sultry weather of midsummer was created by Sirius and it was seen as an evil time, when the high temperatures turned people mad.

Bright, clear days at this time of year mean that cereal crops will be in prime condition by harvest time, which occurs between August and October, and that fruit crops will be perfectly ripened. In the fourteenth century, wet weather in midsummer was an ill omen for the year ahead for similarly practical reasons. Warmth and moisture in combination create a perfect breeding ground for bacteria and in the days before antibiotics, infectious diseases were killers. Damp air in the dog days also meant that preserving meat became impossible: before refrigeration, meat was cured using salt to make it last into the lean winter months, but to obtain salt sea water had to be evaporated slowly in warm, dry conditions; without it meat rotted and people went hungry. In 1315, rains that began in the spring lasted throughout the summer and caused crop failures and salt shortages that resulted in Europe's Great Famine, which caused the deaths of millions of people.

These days we still use the phrase to refer to the long, sultry summer months. We also now use the term 'dog days' to describe any period of stagnation.

THE WORSE
THE PASSAGE THE
MORE WELCOME
THE PORT

In the modern world of global travel the literal meaning of this proverb remains just as true as it was in our maritime past, and the deeper allusion to the journey of life and the relief or satisfaction we feel when we reach the end of a difficult task or period of time chimes with modern experience. Once made, the journey can be viewed in accordance with the French saying, 'What was hard to endure is sweet to recall.'

The nautical English adage, which broadly means the greater the trouble the more appreciated the reward, was recorded by Thomas Fuller, a scholar, writer and doctor who studied at Queens' College, Cambridge, and who practised medicine as well as compiling *Gnomologia: Adagies and Proverbs, Wise Sentences and Witty Sayings*, published in London in 1732. In the preface he writes, '. . . all I dare undertake is to give you a collection of such remarkable sentences and sayings as are usual and useful in conversation and business . . . it has been my constant custom to note down and record whatever I thought of myself, or received from men or books worth preserving.'

'The worse the passage the more welcome the port' would have rung true for eighteenth-century seafarers, who faced cramped conditions and voyages that took months, but it also succinctly expresses something we recognize from our own hard-won experience.

WHEN THE PEACOCK LOUDLY BAWLS

When the peacock loudly bawls
Soon we'll have both rain and squalls.

Peacocks feature frequently in folklore: in Islamic legend a peacock stands guard at the gates of Paradise; in the Middle East they were viewed as the messengers of God; and in pagan mythology they are a symbol of rebirth. In many cultures the 'eyes' at the ends of their feathers were thought to represent the all-seeing eye, which led to the belief that the bird was a powerful prophet.

This saying blends such mythological wisdom with the countryman's careful observation of the reactions of birds and animals to changes in the weather. Peacocks are said to dance and sing when they see rain clouds, though this behaviour occurs frequently throughout the mating season, which begins in spring and ends in early autumn. The key to understanding the origin of this phrase may be the word 'loudly'. Sound travels better through air that is dense with moisture than it does through dry air so before rain the peacock's cry seems louder and travels further than usual.

A squall or short windstorm is also usually preceded by a drop in atmospheric pressure, to which animals are more sensitive than humans. Low pressure of the sort that heralds the arrival of a sudden squall may also be responsible for a bit of extra posturing from peacocks, as they sense the imminent arrival of gusty weather.

THERE IS NO ROSE WITHOUT A THORN

The allegorical symbolism of the rose, with its blend of beauty and spikiness, has earned it mythical status in almost every civilization. Rose petals, rose oil and rose water all feature in Greek, Roman and early European legend; depictions of roses can be found in Egyptian tombs; and in Persia, one of the countries where the flower is thought to have first been cultivated, Sufi poetry records that the rose represented life itself. This saying may in fact have its roots in the ancient Persian proverb 'He who wants a rose must respect the thorn.'

Our version of the phrase was in use in England by the first half of the fifteenth century, when the poet and Benedictine monk John Lydgate, a pupil of Chaucer, wrote a translation of the work of Italian poet Boccaccio, which included the line:

There is no rose . . . in garden, but there be sum thorne.

The Italian proverb *'non c'e rosa senza spine'* is therefore a likely source, though Lydgate is thought to have made his translation from a French paraphrasing of Boccaccio's work, so our proverb may come from the French *'pas de rose sans épine'*. There are subtle variations in interpretations of the phrase; religious readings take from it a lesson that hardship and sacrifice must be endured in order to achieve perfection, while in modern secular usage it is generally read as a warning that all good things have a downside. You may land a dream job – to find that your immediate superior is a vindictive bully; you may move into a beautiful house – to find that you have the proverbial 'neighbours from hell', and so on.

A ROLLING STONE GATHERS NO MOSS

This famous saying is often credited to the first-century BC Roman aphorist Publilius Syrus as his maxim 524 – *Saxum volutum non obducitur musco* – though there is in fact no written record to confirm its provenance. A similar adage appears in one version of *Piers Plowman* (*c.* 1360–87): 'selden Moseþ þe Marbelston þat men ofte treden' ('seldom does the marble-stone that is often trodden on become mossy'), and *Queen Elizabeth's Academy* by Sir Humphrey Gilbert (a proposal he presented to the Queen in 1573 for an academy in London, which still exists today as Gresham College) cites 1460 as a date for 'Syldon mossyth the stone þat oftyn ys tornnyd & wende' – 'Seldom does the stone become mossy that is often turned and rolled.')

It first appeared in the form we recognize today in Erasmus's *Adagia,* published around 1500, which has the line: '*Musco lapis volutus haud obducitur*', meaning 'A stone set rolling is not covered with moss.' The English translation was included in the Tudor playwright John Heywood's 1546 collection of proverbs, *A dialogue conteinyng the nomber in effect of all the prouerbes in the Englishe tongue,* as 'The rollyng stone neuer gatherth mosse.'

For hundreds of years the proverbial meaning was straightforward. Moss grows very slowly from spores, which need time to anchor themselves, so a still, undisturbed stone makes a good foundation for moss to flourish; similarly, a fruitful, productive life can only come from putting down roots and establishing yourself in one place, so if you're a rolling stone, you'll have nothing to show for yourself.

By the early sixteenth century the term 'rolling stone' had become synonymous with vagabond or wastrel and this interpretation still holds. But when legendary Blues musician Muddy Waters labelled himself a Rollin' Stone, there was a section of society that thought it sounded like a good thing to be. By the time the Rolling Stones used Waters's song as their band name, the phrase was associated with being free-spirited and unencumbered by responsibility. Today the phrase is often used as a justification for constant change and chimes with a modern notion that it's preferable not to tie yourself down.

VOWS MADE IN STORMS ARE FORGOTTEN IN CALMS

A modern rendition might be: vows that are made in extreme circumstances are forgotten when the situation normalizes, a sentence which illustrates, by contrast, the lyrical merit of traditional sayings. In his *Works* (published 1629), the puritan Thomas Adams (1583–1652) wrote: 'God had need to take what deuotion he can get at our hands in our misery; for when prosperity returnes, wee forget our vowes.' And Thomas Fuller, the churchman and historian (1608–61), used the proverb in his *Historie of the Holy Warre* (1647), when he remarked of some cardinals, who had vowed never more to take bribes or live 'so viciously' while the Holy Land was under Turkish rule, that 'these mariners' vows ended with the tempest' .

The saying expresses a universal sentiment found in many cultures. The Japanese have a phrase, *'Nodo-moto sugureba asusa wo wasureru'*: 'After it has passed the throat the hotness of it is forgotten.'

A biblical source for the idea of vows made with a view to ensuring a prospective advantage and of vows occasioned by fear of some dreaded calamity was noted in the dramatically illustrated publication *The Sunday at Home: a Family Magazine for Sabbath Reading*: 'The sailors of the ship in which Jonah attempted to flee from God and his duty, we are told "feared the Lord exceedingly, and offered a sacrifice unto the Lord, and made vows" (Jonah i. 16, Authorized King James Bible, 1611). Ever since the days of Jonah, it has been characteristic of this class [sailors] to make sudden vows; for living much on a treacherous element, which is ever liable to be agitated by quick and dangerous storms, when these arise and destruction is imminent the frightened mariner bethinks himself of his neglected duty and makes vows to his god. But alas, how often are the vows made in storms forgotten in calms.'

YOU CAN LEAD A HORSE TO WATER BUT YOU CANNOT MAKE IT DRINK

This well-known aphorism dates back to the twelfth century or earlier, and its moral message was already well established by the time it appeared in a collection of Old English Homilies in 1175 as:

Hwa is thet mei thet hors wettrien the him self nule drinken.

(Who is it that can give water to a horse that won't drink of his own will?)

Unlike most other proverbs in use that early this one appears to have its origins in Old English rather than Latin or Greek, which has led some sources to cite it as the oldest truly English proverb still in use today.

Though not directly biblical, it did have religious significance and was originally used to convey the point that while believers or preachers can do everything in their power to persuade 'sinners' to accept the word of God, the final decision on how to live will always be determined by the will of the individual. These days we still use the phrase in contexts where one person is trying to influence another for their own good, usually by offering advice or providing the circumstances they need in order to do the right thing. In recent years the phrase has even found its way into the modern workplace, where it's employed to convey the frustration of trying to effect change where people or organizations are stuck in their ways.

WE NEVER KNOW THE WORTH OF WATER TILL THE WELL RUNS DRY

This saying appeared as 'When the well's dry, we know the worth of water' in American statesman Benjamin Franklin's annual pamphlet *Poor Richard's Almanack* in 1746, leading many people mistakenly to believe that he coined the phrase. In fact, though Franklin's almanacs do contain many original observations, they also feature lists of established proverbs with which his readers would already have been familiar. This one had been in use for at least a century by the time Franklin recorded it. A Scottish source is likely since the earliest printed version can be found in James Carmichaell's *Proverbs in Scots*, which was published in 1628:

> *Manie wats not quhairof the wel*
> *sauris quhill it fall drie.*
> *(Many notice nothing of how the*
> *well tastes until it falls dry.)*

By 1659 the phrase had made its way south of the border and appeared in James Howell's *Paramoigraphy* (Proverbs). With some English modifications it had become:

Of the Well we see no want, till either dry, or Water skant.

And in 1732 it was included in the physician Thomas Fuller's *Gnomologia*: 'We never know the worth of water till the well is dry.'

The different forms of words do nothing to alter the lesson the phrase teaches, which is to be grateful for all that we have, since we often take the sources of our sustenance for granted until they are suddenly removed and their true value becomes evident.

THE DARKEST HOUR IS THAT BEFORE THE DAWN

This proverb may be most recognizable to today's readers as a song lyric; it appears in Bob Dylan's 'Meet Me in the Morning', along with a number of other American folksongs, and is the title of the Stanley Brothers' country ballad made famous by Emmy-Lou Harris.

It appears to have been printed for the first time in 1650 in *A Pisgah-Sight of Palestine and the Confines Thereof* – a book on biblical history by the English author and churchman Thomas Fuller (1608–61), which includes the line:

It is always darkest just before the Day dawneth.

Fuller was a contemporary of Milton and a theologian, but there is no suggestion that this phrase comes from religious texts. Its origins may in fact be in Gaelic mythology, which often wasn't recorded until long after it had become folklore. In 1858 Irish painter and songwriter Samuel Lover, who wrote two books on rural life in Ireland, noted in his *Songs and Ballads* of 1839:

There is a beautiful saying amongst the Irish peasantry to inspire hope under adverse circumstances: 'Remember,' they say, 'that the darkest hour of all, is the hour before day.'

Unlike many country proverbs there is no scientific foundation for the phrase when it's taken literally – darkness doesn't intensify in the hour before the sunrise, though in contrast to daybreak it may have seemed as if it did. When taken metaphorically, however, it is little more than a truism – when matters cannot get any worse – any darker – they have to start getting better. We still use the phrase to encourage optimism in times of hardship or to comfort people who are in despair.

WHEN THE CAT'S AWAY THE MICE WILL PLAY

Though its exact provenance is unknown, this phrase is believed to have its roots in early Rome since it existed first in Latin. The original version reads:

> *Dum felis dormit, mus*
> *gaudet et exsilit antro.*
> *('When the cat falls asleep, the mouse*
> *rejoices and leaps from the hole.')*

In early fourteenth-century France the rat had displaced the mouse: *'Ou chat na rat regne'* – 'Where there is no cat, the rat is king.' This version gives the best clue to the original meaning, which referred to the rebellious behaviour of the people when their king or ruler was absent for too long.

(The mice danced back for the modern French version: '*Quand le chat n'est pas là, les souris dansent.*')

The saying existed in English round about 1470, collected in the eighteenth-century *Harleian Miscellany or, A Collection of Scarce, Curious, And Entertaining Pamphlets And Tracts* ... : 'The mows lordchypythe [rules] ther a cat ys nawt,' meaning that people will misbehave if rules and leadership are lacking.

By the time the Jacobean playwright Thomas Heywood's domestic tragedy *A Woman Killed with Kindness* was printed in 1607, it was an established enough phrase for him to write: 'There's an old prouerbe, when the cats away, the mouse may play.'

Heywood's play was about adultery and in the context of his story of a husband's betrayal by his guest and his wife, the phrase referred to infidelity behind the back of the master of the house. This is the way the phrase is often used today.

MAKE HAY WHILE THE SUN SHINES

A sixteenth-century proverb advocating action while circumstances are favourable, or seizing an opportunity. It appeared in John Heywood's *Dialogue of Proverbs* in 1546 as part of the following rhyming couplet:

> *Whan the sunne shynth make hey.*
> *Whiche is to say.*
> *Take time whan time cometh, lest*
> *time steale away.*

The phrase appears as 'Yt is well therefore to make hay while the sunne shines' in a 1583 novel, *Philotimus: The Warre between Nature and Fortune,* by Brian Melbancke.

There's no evidence of an earlier version of this phrase existing in other languages so it is thought to be a home-grown homily originating from medieval farming lore. Hay is made from cut grasses, which had to be dried in the fields before they could be baled and stored as animal feed. Dry weather was crucial for a good yield since wet weather could cause the grasses to rot before they were dry enough to store. Using medieval tools, harvesting the hay took several days and predicting the weather several days ahead was almost impossible, so farmers had to take the first opportunity available to them.

The phrase is likely to have been used metaphorically

from the outset and this was certainly the case by 1673, when Richard Head published his glossary of the language of thieves and rogues *The Canting Academy*, and included the line:

She . . . was resolv'd . . . to make Hay whilest the Sun shin'd.

We still use the phrase as a call to act while you can ('while the iron's hot' – see p. 44) , though it can also now refer more explicitly to having fun while you have the chance. There is a reminder of mortality too in its echo of Horace's *carpe diem* ('seize the day').

THE POT CALLING
THE KETTLE
BLACK

This sixteenth-century caution against hypocrisy has its origins in the kitchens of the late Middle Ages. Food was cooked over an open fire and in order that they could withstand the intense heat, pots, kettles and other cooking utensils were all made from the same durable metal – cast iron, which turns black with use. A pot that called a kettle black would therefore be making a criticism that applied equally to itself.

Exactly when this phrase first came into use is difficult to pinpoint but by 1620, when Thomas Shelton translated Cervantes' masterpiece *Don Quixote*, a slightly different version was well known enough to allow him this reference:

> *You are like what is said that the*
> *frying-pan said to the kettle,*
> *'Avant, black-browes.'*

By the end of the seventeenth century the frying pan had been replaced by the pot and in 1693 William Penn, the founder of the state of Pennsylvania, included the saying in the form we still use today in his collection of maxims, *Some Fruits of Solitude*:

For a Covetous Man to inveigh against Prodigality, is for the Pot to call the Kettle black.

An early dictionary of English slang, *A New Dictionary of the Terms Ancient and Modern of the Canting Crew*, compiled by 'B. E.' and published in London around 1698, has a more trenchant version:

'The Pot calls the kettle black A—', when one accuses another of what he is as Deep in himself.

These days the phrase, or sometimes the snappier 'Pot, kettle, black', is still in regular use as a chastisement when people pick on someone for a character trait that they share or a mistake that they have been guilty of themselves.

A BURNT CHILD DREADS THE FIRE

This is a Middle English homily that has been around since the mid-thirteenth century when it appeared in a collection of wise words called *The Proverbs of Hendyng* as: 'Brend child fuir fordredeth.'

The sixteenth-century English writer John Lyly used the phrase in his 1580 work *Euphues and His England*:

> *A burnt childe dreadeth the fire . . .*
> *Thou mayst happely forsweare thy*
> *selfe, but thou shalt neuer delude me.*

The message is clear: a person becomes distrustful of something that – or someone who – has harmed them. In the Middle Ages people lived in close proximity to fire as it was the only source of heat and light available. A well-managed fire used for cooking and warmth was certainly something to take care around but not usually something to dread. A young child, however, might be attracted to the flames and, unaware that fire burns, reach out for them.

Around the same time, a similar French proverb, *'chat échaudé craint l'eau froide'* (the scalded cat fears cold water) was translated into English, appearing in 1732 in Thomas Fuller's *Gnomologia* as 'Scalded Cats fear even cold Water,' reminding us that the dread might be excessive, perhaps to the point of being wholly irrational.

An early adage carrying the same message is to be found in Æsop's fable about the Cat and the Mice, translated by William Caxton in 1484: 'He that hath ben ones begyled by somme other ought to kepe hym wel fro[m] the same.'

'Once bitten, twice shy' is a rather more succinct way of putting it. It first appeared in this form in *Folk Phrases of Four Counties* by G. G. Northall, published in 1894, and remains in frequent use.

This maxim has a similar domestic tone as the cautions about burnt children and scalded cats: keep away from fire, hot water and fierce animals . . . there is much to be wary of in life.

STRIKE WHILE THE IRON'S HOT

Used to encourage people to take action promptly when they have the best chance of success, this thirteenth-century proverb has its roots in medieval blacksmiths' forges. Iron had to be heated to high temperatures in furnaces to make it pliable enough to make tools, weapons and cooking utensils. The blacksmith would strike the white-hot iron with a hammer to re-shape it and had only a brief window of time in which to work before the iron cooled and became rigid again.

The saying – which could be compared with the agricultural 'Make hay while the sun shines' – was applied to any situation that required action to be taken when the circumstances were most favourable and where hesitation might cause an opportune moment to be lost. The earliest example of the phrase in print can be found in the second of Chaucer's *Canterbury Tales*, 'The Tale of Melibee', written in 1386:

> *Whil that iren is hoot, men sholden smyte.*

It is probable, though, that its inclusion in the *Canterbury Tales* helped to popularize the phrase, which is thought to have originated in France. Chaucer's twenty-four tales were some of the first works of literature to be written in the language spoken by the people who read them – English – and they were so popular in their day that Chaucer was invited to read them to the King.

NO MAN CAN SERVE TWO MASTERS

This proverb comes from the Bible:

> *No man can serve two masters: for either he will hate the one, and love the other; or else he will hold to the one, and despise the other. Ye cannot serve God and mammon.*
> *(Matthew 6:24)*

Early use of the phrase stayed true to this religious context and it was applied to those who valued the trappings of wealth over piety.

The lines quoted above follow a paragraph dissuading man from gathering up treasures on Earth (where they will be corroded by rust and stolen by thieves) in favour of laying up treasures in heaven. With the word mammon interpreted as meaning money, the lesson Jesus was teaching is clear: we should value the riches of heaven rather than material wealth.

In the New Testament, however, Mammon is personified as an idol or deity representing greed and avarice, so the words spoke against the worshipping of false gods as well as warning against succumbing to the base desire to accumulate wealth.

These days the saying is employed to describe any situation where there is a conflict of interest or where loyalties are divided. We're especially fond of applying it to high-profile political figures who claim to be representing the public whilst earning extra cash or status by serving the interests of big businesses.

DON'T LOOK A GIFT HORSE IN THE MOUTH

This ancient phrase can be traced to the writing of fourth-century Latin churchman St Jerome, who used it in his scholarly commentary of St Paul's Epistle to the Ephesians in around AD 400. His words translate as 'Don't inspect the teeth of a gift horse,' which gives a clue as to the meaning of the current phrase. Examining a horse's teeth is the best way to assess its age as horses' teeth grow constantly to cope with their high-fibre diet. A young horse is of greater value than an old one so to look into the mouth of a horse that had been given as a gift would be, rather rudely, to seek to put a price on the present you'd received.

St Jerome was using what was probably already a well-established aphorism to instruct people to accept gifts graciously and appreciate the intention behind them rather than their monetary worth.

The phrase was recorded in its modern form in John Heywood's *Dialogue of Proverbs* in 1546:

No man ought to looke a geuen hors in the mouth.

The phrase has been linked to the mythological Trojan horse, which was delivered to the gates of Troy as a gift from the Greeks around 1184 BC, but which concealed a Greek army (including two spies in its mouth) that defeated the Trojans. The link is erroneous – looking into the mouth of the Trojan horse might have meant a jab in the eye from a Greek dagger at best – but the tale of the Trojan horse is the origin of another adage: 'Fear the Greeks bearing gifts' (Laocoön's warning to the Trojans in Virgil's *Aeneid* : *Timeo Danaos, et dona ferentes* – 'I fear the Greeks, even when they are bringing gifts').

THEY THAT DANCE MUST PAY THE FIDDLER

A mid-seventeenth-century saying to remind you that you must be prepared to pay for any service that you make use of. Dances were one of the most popular forms of entertainment from the sixteenth century onwards and there were dancing events that appealed to all sections of society, from the rural country dance to the high-society ball. While musicians who played at the latter were paid by the host of the party, at less formal dances it was customary for the fiddler to earn his living through donations from the guests who had enjoyed his performance. In *Taylors Feast* (1638) by the seventeenth-century writer John Taylor, the phrase is used literally but also makes reference to the fact that it was a well-known saying:

> *One of the Fidlers said, Gentlemen,*
> *I pray you to remember the Musicke*
> *[musicians], you have given us*
> *nothing yet . . . Alwayes those that*
> *dance must pay the Musicke.*

In 1837, Abraham Lincoln demonstrated how the phrase

could be used in a political setting to make a case against the spending of state money on resolving private disputes:

It is an old maxim, and a very sound one, that he that dances should always pay the fiddler. Now, sir, in the present case, if any gentlemen whose money is a burden to them, choose to lead off a dance, I am decidedly opposed to the people's money being used to pay the fiddler.

An argument that makes the phrase seem every bit as relevant today as it was in Lincoln's day.

***

A similar saying, possibly derived from it, and with roughly the same meaning but reversing the roles, is:

He who pays the piper calls the tune.

The meaning is clear – the person who is paying chooses what is to be done and how. Surprisingly perhaps, the earliest record of it is as recent as 1895 when *The Daily News* of 18 December stated that 'Londoners had paid the piper, and should choose the tune.'

THERE'S NO SMOKE WITHOUT FIRE

This phrase is proof that the rumour mill has been running since the ancient civilizations. The Roman playwright Plautus (*c.* 254–184 BC), who was famous for his use of proverbs in his writing, included in his comedy *Curculio* the line:

> **Flamma fumo est proxima.**
> (*The flame is right next to the smoke.*)

It meant then as it does now, that rumours don't exist without a source, and that the source is often the truth. From translations of Plautus's work came the thirteenth-century French phrase '*nul feu est sens fumee ne fumee sens feu*,' which translates as: no fire is without smoke, nor smoke without fire. By the fourteenth century, the saying existed in Middle English – and in Scots, appearing in the long narrative poem on Robert the Bruce and other Scottish heroes by the poet and churchman John Barbour:

And thair may no man fire sa covir,
[Bot] low or reyk [flame or smoke]
sall it discovir.

It was readily integrated into British folklore and later travelled with the early settlers to the US, where the phrase now more commonly exists in the modernized form 'Where there's smoke, there's fire.' We use it today to imply that even when an individual or organization denies whatever scandalous behaviour has been attributed to them, it's rare for gossip to start circulating without there being some degree of truth behind the tale.

EVERY DOG
HAS HIS DAY

This saying has its roots in Ancient Greece and was recorded for the first time in AD 95 by Greek biographer Plutarch as 'Even a dog gets his revenge.' One notion about its origins, expounded by Erasmus in his *Adagia* in 1500, is that it was coined after the death of the Greek playwright Euripides, in his seventies, in 406 BC. There are several theories about exactly how Euripides died, but one story has him visiting the King of Macedonia and being mauled to death by a pack of dogs that had been set on him by a rival.

The phrase was used to convey the idea that if even a creature as lowly as a dog can overthrow a renowned and well-connected figure, then the most humble men should have faith that their chance for retribution against their oppressors will come. It was used as a form of encouragement to the downtrodden and as a warning to anyone who abused their power over others.

The version we're more familiar with today appeared for the first time in English in Richard Taverner's translation of Erasmus's *Adagia* (second edition, 1545), where it appeared as:

A dogge hath a day.

The phrase was picked up by John Heywood, appearing in his *Dialogue of Proverbs* (1546) as:

As euery man saith, a dog hath a daie.

Elizabeth I used it in 1550:

Notwithstanding, as a dog hath a day, so may I perchance have time to declare it in deeds.

And Shakespeare popularized it at the turn of the century with his now famous couplet in *Hamlet*:

Let Hercules himself do what he may, The cat will mew and dog will have his day.

These days the phrase has lost much of its malice and is often used to suggest that everyone will get their chance at success.

DON'T PUT ALL YOUR EGGS IN ONE BASKET

In the most straightforward of terms, carrying all your eggs in one basket is clearly a risky strategy. One trip on an uneven country road could cause that basket to slip from your arm and all your eggs would be cracked. The Italians seem to have been the first to see the sense in splitting a valuable load to avoid such a catastrophe and some sources cite a 1662 translation of an Italian phrase 'To put all ones Eggs in a Paniard' as the origin of our own version. It means don't invest all your money, time or efforts in just one enterprise in case it fails and leaves you with nothing. It's safer, the phrase suggests, to divide your resources so that if one metaphorical basket overturns, you've got several others that are still secure.

In Samuel Palmer's book of proverbs (*Moral essays on some of the most curious . . . English, Scotch, and foreign proverbs*, published in 1710), the phrase appears as 'Don't venture all your eggs in one basket', which elucidates its meaning more fully than the more modern wording if we take 'venture' to mean 'risk' or 'gamble'.

Today the phrase is synonymous with 'hedging your bets', a saying also coined in the late seventeenth century. It refers to the practice of placing several small bets with a range of lenders in order to offset a larger bet – putting figurative hedges round them to protect and limit them – and basically means keeping your options open.

HE THAT GOES BAREFOOT MUST NOT PLANT THORNS

Though it may sound like a straightforward piece of advice for gardeners who like to feel the grass between their toes, this phrase has been recognized as a proverb since the late sixteenth century. In 1611 it appeared in print for the first time in *A dictionarie of the French and English tongues*, compiled by the lexicographer Randle Cotgrave. Alongside his translations, he included a number of proverbs, many of which existed in both languages, to show how the word might be put to use. Under *pied*, he put :

> *He that will bare-foot goe must plant no thornes.*

Fuller keeps it brief in *Gnomologia* (1732):

> *'Barefoot must not go among Thorns.'*

Thorns were as much of an irritation to the peasants of old as they are to today's gardeners, but the consequences of getting a thorn embedded in the skin were far graver in the days before tetanus jabs, chemical disinfectants and antibiotics.

The phrase does seem to be rooted in the fairly obvious dangers of stepping on a thorn but was used figuratively as a way of expressing the view that people shouldn't create situations that they're not equipped to deal with. Feel free to plant thorns if you've got a sensible pair of thick-soled boots, a modern version of the phrase might go, but stick to artificially cultivated thornless roses if you prefer to float around with your shoes and socks off. The phrase is similar in essence to another old proverb: those in glass houses shouldn't throw stones.

First recorded in John Clarke's *Parœmiologia Anglo-Latina*, published in 1639, is a Latin proverb which reads 'Where ever a man dwell he shall be sure to have a thorne-bush near his doore' – an indication that few stations in life were likely to be entirely free from trouble. When he included it in his *Collection of Proverbs* in 1678, the naturalist John Ray added as a practical aside the more literal difficulty of avoiding thorn bushes by explaining that there 'are few places in England where a man can dwell, but he shall have one near him.'

CURIOSITY KILLED THE CAT

This phrase warning against inquisitiveness is relatively modern in this form, only finding its way into print just before the end of the nineteenth century. The proverb it originates from, however, has a much longer history. 'Care killed the cat', where 'care' meant anxiety or grief, was already in regular use by the time the English playwright Ben Jonson used it in his comedy *Every Man in his Humour* in 1598:

> *Helter skelter, hang sorrow, care'll kill a Cat, up-tails all, and a Louse for the Hangman.*

Medieval medicine was based on the belief that the body contained four humours – black bile, yellow bile, phlegm and blood, which must be correctly balanced for good health to be maintained. Melancholia (characterized by sadness and anxiety – or 'care') was thought to be the result of too much black bile, which was damaging to the health.

The earliest printed evidence of the change from 'care' to 'curiosity' is thought to be in the Gaveston *Daily News* of 1898: 'It is said that once "curiosity killed a Thomas cat."'

Cats have a strong presence in British folklore; they

were thought to bring bad luck through their association with witches and the myth that they have nine lives may have given rise to ideas about what kinds of behaviour might actually kill them. With the template of the earlier phrase already in place, cats' tendency to explore every nook and cranny, including narrow spaces and perilously high ones, made them useful in a metaphor for the dangers of concerning yourself with other people's business.

THERE'S A BLACK SHEEP IN EVERY FLOCK

Since the late eighteenth century this phrase has been used to refer to the presence in every family or community of one disreputable character or misfit. The wool trade had been a lynchpin of the British economy since medieval times when every landowner, even the relatively poor owners of tiny smallholdings, would have raised as many sheep as their acreage allowed.

Black sheep are rarer than white (just common enough for most flocks to include at least one) and can be born unexpectedly into a white flock since the gene that determines the black colour is recessive. Their rarity didn't make them valuable to sheep farmers, though, because their wool can't be dyed, so they were usually unwelcome arrivals. They were also regarded by many as a sign of more widespread bad luck (black-woolled twin lambs were especially bad news) as in English folklore the colour black is associated with the Devil. Christian demonologists believed that demons often took the form of animals whose skin or fur was black, hence the widespread distrust of black cats (confusingly, also seen as bringing good luck), as well as the view that a black sheep was in some way a bad one.

These superstitions combined with another widespread eighteenth-century view – that conformity was fundamentally a good thing – to cement this phrase as an often repeated homily whenever a rogue relation threatened to bring shame or embarrassment on the family.

LADYBIRD, LADYBIRD, FLY AWAY HOME

This traditional rhyme dates back to 1744 when it was published in an anthology of nursery rhymes. Numerous versions exist, the most well known in the UK being:

Ladybird, ladybird, fly away home,
Your house is on fire and your children
are gone,
All except one,
And her name is Ann,
And she hid under the frying pan.

In America the verse is rather more bleak:

Ladybug, ladybug, fly away home,
Your house is on fire,
Your children shall burn!

Legend has it that during a plague of plant-destroying insects in the Middle Ages, desperate farmers prayed to the Virgin Mary for help and their prayers were answered by a swarm of ladybirds, which preserved the crops by eating all the invaders. In recognition of this they became known as 'lady beetles', and later 'ladybirds'. Or, in the US, 'ladybugs', and it was seen as bad luck to kill one.

Some sources suggest the rhyme was taught to children to encourage them to treat ladybirds gently as they were also helpful to farmers because of their diet of more destructive insects. Others say it was recited by the farmers themselves as they attempted to shoo the useful creatures off their land before they began the routine practice of preparing their fields for the following year's crops by setting them alight, or tried to rid their crops of other insects by smoking them out. These days we say the rhyme and make a wish as we blow a ladybird off our clothing.

MIGHT AS WELL BE HANGED FOR A SHEEP AS A LAMB

This proverb was first recorded in 1678 in John Ray's *Collection of Proverbs* as:

As good be hang'd for an old sheep as a young lamb.

But it is likely to have been in use since at least the start of the seventeenth century as the belief it expounds was described in a 1662 commentary on the Biblical parable of the Rich Fool by clergyman Nehemiah Rogers, who wrote: 'As some desperate Wretches, Who despairing of life still act the more villainy, giving this desperate Reason of it, As good be hanged for a great deal, as for a little.'

The saying itself is a reference to the harsh British penal system which attached the death penalty (or at the very least, deportation to Australia) to a list of crimes which today we might consider minor. The theft of goods worth more than one shilling carried a death sentence, as did stealing sheep, regardless of the size or age of the animal. The phrase makes a mockery of the efficacy of such draconian penalties by pointing out that rather than deterring those desperate enough to risk death in order to steal a lamb, they simply encouraged hungry thieves to set their sights on the largest sheep they could find.

By the time the law was finally reformed in the 1820s the phrase was well established as a proverb and is still used to suggest that if the consequences of your actions will be the same no matter what kind of risk you take, you may as well make it a big one.

MARES' TAILS AND MACKEREL SCALES

Mares' tails and mackerel scales
Make lofty ships carry low sails.

The system of Latin cloud names weather forecasters use today was created by English pharmacist Luke Howard in 1803. Before then (and since in many parts of the world) amateur observers of the weather used traditional names derived from the way the clouds looked. Mares' tails are what we now know as cirrus clouds, and were given their name because they often resemble the flowing tail of a horse as it runs. They're the most common form of high-level cloud and because they are usually found at heights above 20,000 feet, where air pressure is low, they are usually very thin and wispy – the Latin word *cirrus* means 'curl'. Mares' tails are made up of ice crystals that form when the water droplets in them freeze; they usually occur in fair weather, but can precede a storm, especially when seen, as the rhyme suggests, alongside 'mackerel scales'.

Mackerel scales are altocumulus clouds, which are small, rounded white puffs that join together to form a rippling blanket of puffs, or 'scales', in the sky. Their appearance is caused by the influence of shifting wind directions typical of an advancing low-pressure system that usually brings stormy weather.

These cloud formations were particularly useful to sailors of large vessels who would have had to lower their sails in preparation for gusty weather.

MANY HANDS MAKE LIGHT WORK

The most popular proverbs are often those that sound so simple you could have made them up yourself if only you'd been able to find the right turn of phrase. This one was among the 4,658 adages compiled by the great medieval scholar Erasmus by the time of his death from dysentery in 1536. His version read *Multae manus onus levius reddunt*, which was translated as:

Many hands make a burden lighter.

It's obvious but also somehow so much wiser than anything we could come up with to convey the same meaning today. The homily was previously translated into Middle English in the early fourteenth century in a poem called *Sir Bevis of Hampton*, a metrical romance based on a French original about the eponymous legendary hero which featured a formidable giant called Ascopard. The tale included the line:

Ascopard be strong and sterk,
Mani hondes maketh light werk!

The phrase was further popularized when various printed editions of the romance were printed in the sixteenth and early seventeenth centuries, delivering this very ancient piece of wisdom to a mass 'modern' audience.

It was particularly well tailored to the needs of British agricultural workers and early American settlers, who spent most of their working lives engaged in manual labour that couldn't have been completed without a team effort. Today we use the phrase most frequently when asking for help with some onerous task which would seem insurmountable without someone to share the load.

Though, of course, there is a counter-argument: as *The Observer* of 11 February 1923 complained:

What is the use of saying that 'Many hands make light work' when the same copy-book tells you that 'Too many cooks spoil the broth'?

JACK OF ALL TRADES, MASTER OF NONE

From the Middle Ages, the word 'jack' was interchangeable with 'man'. Medieval townsfolk would have used the term in the same way that we might when forced by a DIY crisis to 'get a man in to do the job'. More precisely, a 'jack' was a menial labourer who touted himself from door to door looking for manual work, so a jack of all trades was a labourer who could be employed in any of the basic trades required by the households of the Middle Ages.

The phrase 'Jack of all trades' was used in its Latin

form to begin with – as in a little rant by Robert Greene in 1592 against a rival writer, an 'upstart crow ... an absolute *Johannes factotum*, is in his owne conceit'; the rival writer was William Shakespeare. In 1612, the phrase appeared in English in *Essays and Characters of a Prison and Prisoners*, a social commentary on the appalling conditions in British prisons, by Geffray Mynshul, thought to have been detained at Gray's Inn prison as a debtor. He mentions 'Some broken Cittizen, who hath plaid Jack-of-all-trades'. At the time, however, the term was generally not derogatory, implying as it did a wide range of skills and abilities of which any working man would be proud. But a second, more disparaging part of the saying was beginning to circulate. In 1677, a Martin Clifford said of some of John Dryden's poetry that they were like a 'Jack of all Trades Shop, they have Variety, but nothing of value'.

And in 1785 Charles Lucas – apothecary, physician and politician (so a bit of a jack of all trades himself) – wrote of the 'Druggist' in Britain as being 'a Jack of all trades, and in truth, master of none'.

The phrase came to mean that to maintain a wide range of abilities the quality of each must be compromised, and it is this version that has stood the test of time. On occasion, people might still be heard describing themselves as 'a bit of a jack of all trades' when asked their occupation, but we would usually assume that they were either unemployed or dodging the question to avoid prosecution.

AS YOU SOW, SO YOU SHALL REAP

This teaching is a modern version of the words, 'Be not deceived; God is not mocked: for whatsoever a man soweth, that shall he also reap' (Galatians, 6:7). The Epistle of Paul to the Galatians (ninth book of the New Testament) was written to a number of Early Christian communities in the Roman province of Galatia in central Anatolia, exhorting the Galatian believers to stand fast in the Christian faith. The teaching means that the personal consequences of your actions are in proportion to your good or bad intentions towards others, and those consequences will come back to you as payment for your deeds (see also 'Curses, like chickens, come home to roost', p. 147). This moral view is very similar to the concept of karma in Hinduism and Buddhism.

Karma in Sanskrit means 'action' or 'doing'. Whatever one does, says or thinks is a karma, and according to the Vedas (the sacred Hindu texts), if one sows goodness, one will reap goodness; if one sows evil, one will reap evil. Like many ancient teachings, the powerful biblical allegory is rooted in our agrarian past where the sowing of seed inexorably determined the nature of the harvest to follow. In Christian terms, these words are usually understood to constitute a moral precept, teaching the importance of goodness and the inevitable personal consequences of doing evil. However, in the Eastern religions of Hinduism and Buddhism, karma is a natural law believed to be inherent in the nature of being, rather than a moral adage.

In Randle Cotgrave's 1611 English–French dictionary, he includes 'He that sows thistles shall reap prickles.' A rather more sombre version is 'They that sow the wind, shall reap the whirlwind,' an allusion to Hosea 8:7: 'They have sown the wind, and they shall reap the whirlwind.'

We still use the phrase today, often in the more modern form 'reap what you sow.'

NE'ER CAST A CLOUT TILL MAY BE OUT

This sage piece of advice for coping with the dramatic seasonal differences in British weather is likely to have been in regular use since well before it first appeared in print in 1732. In Old English the word 'clout' meant patch of cloth, such as might be used to cover a hole in a worn-out piece of clothing. By the fifteenth century it had broadened to mean garment or clothing in general, so this was a warning against discarding your winter layer until the end of the month of May.

Some sources offer an alternative interpretation of the words 'till May be out', suggesting that 'May' refers to the flowers of the hawthorn tree, which are traditionally known by that name. During a century of agricultural enclosures beginning in 1750, pre-eminent British botanist Oliver Rackham estimates that 200,000 miles of hawthorn hedge were planted, making the May blossom a well-known feature of the countryside.

May blossom comes out in late April, early May, coinciding with the start of warmer weather, which lends credence to the idea that this was the sign country folk should wait for before removing their winter layers, but most academic interpretations side with the idea that the reference is to the end of the month of May.

They are supported by a similar French proverb from the same period which also mentions April, perhaps in order to accommodate the slightly warmer climate of mainland Europe:

En avril, ne te découvre pas d'un fil; en mai, fais ce qui te plaît.
(*In April, do not shed a single thread; in May, do as you please.*)

ONE FOR THE ROOK

One for the rook, one for the crow,
One to rot and one to grow.

An old smallholders' saying that was recited since at least the late eighteenth century as they sowed their seeds, and which exists in several forms, including:

One for the mouse, one for the crow,
One to rot and one to grow.

And:

One for wind and one for crow,
One to die and one to grow.

All refer to the fact that in small vegetable gardens it was usual to sow seeds broadcast, which means scattering them widely on the surface of the soil and then gently raking the ground to draw a thin layer of earth over them. The seeds stayed near the surface leaving them vulnerable to birds and animals and to the wind, which could cause such severe damage to seedlings that many kitchen gardeners recommend growing fragile plants between wooden stakes to protect them from damaging gusts.

These days birds can be kept off newly sown seeds by breathable protective covers, but in the mid-1800s, when the phrase first appeared in print, farmers had to accept that a share of what they put in the ground would be donated to the wildlife. Mice are particularly fond of eating young bean pods and germinating seeds, and two versions of the rhyme express the risk that a percentage of crops will die or rot. This was especially true of vegetables, which are water- and nutrient-hungry and need constant care and attention throughout their growing period. Too much water in the soil could be equally damaging and cause a seed to rot, while low temperatures could mean that some plants die in the ground.

IF A CIRCLE FORMS ROUND THE MOON, 'TWILL RAIN OR SNOW SOON

Much of the myth and legend that finds its way into folklore was concerned with finding ways to use the natural world to help people plan their lives. The moon features in many old sayings because, without understanding why, medieval man recognized that it had some influence on what was happening on Earth.

According to folklore the waxing and waning of the moon causes a monthly increase and lessening of the earth's water content, with the time of greatest moisture occurring when the moon is full. The different phases of the moon were thought to be influential in whether crops would thrive or fail; a full moon was favoured for harvesting moisture-rich plants, while root vegetables were planted when farmers could see the dark side of the moon.

The presence of a halo or ring around the moon was seen as a sign that bad weather would follow, and as early storm warnings go, it was fairly accurate. The halo occurs when moonlight (reflected light from the invisible sun) is refracted through clouds of six-sided crystals of ice high in the upper atmosphere. The crystals act as prisms and as the light hits them, they reflect the light at such an angle that it appears to form a ring.

The clouds of frozen water droplets, known as cirro-stratus cloud, often precede an approaching warm front and the area of low pressure that accompanies it, conditions which often result in rain or, if the temperature is cool enough, snow.

SNEEZE ON MONDAY

Sneeze on Monday, sneeze for fun
Sneeze on Tuesday, meet someone
Sneeze on Wednesday, get a letter
Sneeze on Thursday, get something
better
Sneeze on Friday, sneeze in sorrow
Sneeze on Saturday, see friends
tomorrow
Sneeze on Sunday, bad luck for a
week.

Sneezing has always been the subject of superstition. The tradition of saying 'bless you' when someone sneezes came about because it used to be believed that a sneeze caused your soul to leave your body for a moment, which could leave it vulnerable to being snatched away by the Devil if someone near by didn't counteract his diabolical powers with a blessing. In Catholic tradition the sneeze was thought to be an evil spirit being expelled from someone's body and the sneezer needed blessing for their bravery in defeating it, while Irish folklore has it that your disembodied soul might be snatched by the pixie-like Little People if someone didn't bless you.

This rhyme illustrates the way sneezes were also used to predict future events, which was a popular notion in the days when planning ahead couldn't be facilitated by telephone or email. Friday apart, sneezes from Monday to Saturday were all auspicious and promised something of interest in the week ahead. But by far the most common superstitions were linked in some way to bad luck, either how to predict it or how to fend it off, and sneezing on the Lord's day wasn't good news. These days we don't make much of the day of the week on which we sneeze, but we do still say 'bless you.'

IF BIRDS FLY LOW, THEN RAIN WE SHALL KNOW

This saying is often preceded by another rhyming couplet: 'Birds fly high, clear blue sky', and was used as a way of predicting the onset of wet weather by farmers who depended on rain at the right times of year to hydrate their crops and yield them a good harvest.

Birds were respected for their close attunement with the climate, and their behaviour was closely observed for hints of what kind of weather lay ahead. Much of their flying behaviour is determined by air pressure, and weather lore that is based on changes in air pressure has scientific reasons behind it and is genuinely useful in making short-term weather forecasts.

Birds really do fly lower in the sky before rain because wet weather is associated with low pressure, which makes the air thinner and more difficult for birds to fly in. The flight patterns of insects are affected in the same way and it may be that birds are brought closer yet to the ground by the descent of their prey.

Another piece of folklore says if rooks' nests are built high in the treetops it will be a fine summer; while if they're closer to the ground the summer will be wet and cold, though this is more likely to be to do with the amount of wind at the time of nest-building than the tell-tale drop in pressure that signals storms.

DON'T COUNT YOUR CHICKENS BEFORE THEY'VE HATCHED

This phrase has been in use since at least the mid-sixteenth century and for many medieval farmers and smallholders it would have had literal as well as metaphorical relevance. The sale of livestock was an important source of income and it must have been tempting to calculate what your budget might be for the following month based on the number of eggs you hoped would have hatched by market day. But eggs are the perfect ingredient for this kind of allegory because for them to hatch successfully conditions have to be exactly right; the rooster needs to be young and virile; the hens have to sit on the eggs so that the temperature stays high enough for the chicks to develop, and the humidity levels have to be higher than average. With all these factors at play it isn't unusual for a number of eggs not to hatch, and in the days before incubators, unhatched eggs were even more common.

The wise words first appeared in print in the poet Thomas Howell's *New Sonnets and Pretty Pamphlets* (1570), which adds an additional line to emphasize this lesson:

Counte not thy Chickens that unhatched be,

Waye wordes as winde, till thou finde certaintee.

These days we abbreviate the phrase to 'Don't count your chickens' and still use it for advocating caution when assessing one's assets. We also use it to explain our own reluctance to assume success before we're sure of it by saying 'I don't want to count my chickens'. More recent US folklore offers the alternative 'Don't go selling the hide while the bear remains in the hole.'

A LEAP YEAR IS NEVER A GOOD SHEEP YEAR

Superstitions about leap years abound and understanding the power of proverbs like this one requires an insight into how we came to have an extra day added to our calendar in the first place. The first leap year occurred in 46 BC with the creation of the Julian calendar, named after Julius Caesar, who reformed the Roman calendar to tally with the natural cycle of the seasons, which had been observed since ancient times to be roughly 365¼ days long. He divided the year into twelve months, with an extra day added to February every fourth year, but a miscalculation meant that leap days were in fact added every third year and the calendar gradually moved out of sync with the astronomical solstices and equinoxes.

In 1582, Pope Gregory XIII established the widespread use of the Gregorian calendar, which kept the addition of a leap day to every fourth year. Despite the fact that the extra day was intended to align the calendar more closely to the rhythms of the planet, many rural people felt that it was tinkering with nature.

Their suspicion of the changes was exacerbated by the removal of ten days from the month of October in the year the Gregorian calendar was introduced. The measure was deeply unpopular with the people, some of whom believed it would cost them ten days of their lives, and there were widespread protests against the changes. They believed that it could throw the cycles of crop growing and livestock rearing out of kilter, thus reducing the number of lambs born each spring.

IF YOU RUN AFTER TWO HARES YOU'LL CATCH NEITHER

This warning against dividing your efforts between two tasks rather than focusing on one was among those collected by Erasmus in his *Adagia* of 1500. The Latin version goes: *'Duos insequens lepores, neutrum capit,'* which translates as 'He who chases two hares catches neither.'

Hares were eaten regularly by the Greeks and Romans and were an important part of the medieval diet. Hare coursing, where hares are hunted with packs of dogs, is one of the oldest field sports in Europe so the phrase resonated with the aristocracy as well as with the peasantry, though the latter were severely punished if they were caught killing or eating a hare that belonged to the Lord of the Manor.

The first example of the phrase in print appeared in 1509 in an English translation of German humanist Sebastian Brant's satire of fifteenth-century folly the *Narrenschiff* (*Ship of Fools*, originally published in 1494), which says: 'A fole is he . . . Whiche with one haunde tendyth [intends] to take two harys in one instant.'

The book was one of the most successful publications of its age and is likely to have been responsible for the continued popularity of the phrase. The proverb would also have appealed to the medieval belief in hares as representatives of cunning and artifice. Countless folktales tell of duplicitous hares who lead men astray and later reveal themselves to be witches in disguise, cementing the notion that to catch one requires one's full and undivided attention.

HE THAT PLANTS A TREE PLANTS FOR POSTERITY

With the vast majority of the population depending on the product of their own kitchen gardens for food, it was seen as a selfless act of kindness towards future generations to devote time and space to planting a tree that wouldn't yield fruit in your own lifetime.

A Latin version of the phrase, which appeared in Cicero's discourse on old age *Cato Major*, is proof of an enduring belief in the sentiment:

Serit arbores, quae alteri saeclo prosint.
('He plants trees, which will be of use to another age.')

The version in Fuller's *Gnomologia* (1732) is rather heartwarming: 'He that plants Trees loves others besides himself.' Fuller also included in that collection the similar 'He who plants a Walnut-Tree, expects not to eat of the Fruit.'

The form we're more used to is employed by Scottish poet and essayist Alexander Smith in his countryside-praising prose work *Dreamthorpe*, published in 1863: 'My oaks are but saplings; but what undreamed-of English kings will they not outlive? A man does not plant a tree for himself; he plants it for posterity.'

Modern readers may be more familiar with a later version of the phrase from the seventeenth century: 'Walnuts and pears you plant for your heirs', which refers to the particularly slow-growing walnut and pear trees, which can take many years to reach maturity.

The phrase was used metaphorically whenever people wanted to convey the point that they were working towards a long-term goal and these days may be heard simply as a sigh of 'walnuts and pears' when parents talk about the lengths they will go to for their children's future.

FIGHT FIRE
WITH FIRE

The idea that in order to defend yourself successfully against attack you must be prepared to use the same methods and weapons, or go to the same extremes, as your enemy, has probably existed since organized fighting began. The phrase 'to fight fire with fire' could be a reference to firearms, even very early ones, but could equally be a reference to fire itself. An early fourteenth-century French phrase states *'lung feu doit estaindre lautre'* – 'one fire must put out another.'

There is no record as to when it was found that one fire can stop another by consuming the oxygen and other fuel – given the right conditions – but Shakespeare was pleased with the metaphoric possibilities, which he used several times. In *Romeo and Juliet* (1592), Benvolio urges Romeo to go to a ball where he can meet other nice girls and get over Rosaline, his first love: 'Tut, man, one fire burns out another's burning.'

And in *King John* (1595), Shakespeare wrote:

> *Be stirring as the time;*
> *be fire with fire;*
> *Threaten the threatener*
> *and outface the brow*
> *Of bragging horror . . .*

Again, in 1608, in *Coriolanus*: 'One fire drives out one fire; one nail, one nail.'

Other versions of the phrase were recorded in the seventeenth and eighteenth centuries, but it is Shakespeare who popularized the saying.

In the 1800s, the phrase was used in its literal sense by the early American settlers, who turned to the technique now common in managing bush fires of lighting a small backfire when forest fires threatened to destroy their settlements. This helped consolidate the use of the phrase in the US, as evidenced by American author Henry Tappan in his 1852 memoir *A Step from the New World to the Old, and Back Again*:

> *Smoking was universal among the men; generally cigars, not fine Havanas, but made of Dutch tobacco, and to me not very agreeable. I had some Havanas with me, and so I lighted one to make an atmosphere for myself: as the trappers on the prairies fight fire with fire, so I fought tobacco with tobacco.*

The phrase is still in regular use on both sides of the Atlantic, though these days we often use it to validate the use of violence in cases of self-defence or to justify sinking to the levels of our rivals in dirty sports matches or office spats.

A BIRD IN THE HAND IS WORTH TWO IN THE BUSH

The concept of this adage – that the possession of one valuable item is of greater worth than the *chance* of possessing two such items, or that a certainty is better than an uncertainty even if the latter is of more value – is clear.

It is believed by some to have its origins in medieval hunting, though there is no evidence as to whether the reference is to the superior value of a trained raptor in the hand in comparison with two hunted birds hiding in the bush, or indeed in comparison with two birds of prey at liberty, or to the superior value of any bird in the hand to a pair deep in the undergrowth or high in the sky. A Latin proverb that would seem to support the latter interpretation is '*Plus valet in manibus passer, quam in nubibus anser*' – 'More valuable is a sparrow in the hands than a goose in the clouds.'

An early precursor (fifth century BC) may be found in Æsop's fable about the nightingale and the hawk. A nightingale, struggling in the hawk's talons, desperately tries to argue that it is so small it wouldn't satisfy the hawk's hunger and should be allowed to go free so that the hawk can pursue larger birds. To no avail; the hawk's reply is clear: 'Not I, for I have been on the watch for you all day and I am not foolish enough to give up a certainty for an uncertainty.'

The phrase as it is known today can be found as early as the thirteenth century in Latin: *plus valet in manibus avis unica quam dupla silvis*, which translates as 'more valuable is a single bird in the hands than twice as many in the woods.'

Possibly the earliest English version in print is to be found in John Capgrave's *Life of St Katherine* (*c.*1450): 'It is more sekyr [certain] a byrd in your fest, than to haue three in the sky a-boue.' It quickly became popular – and a number of versions were collected during the sixteenth and seventeenth centuries, generally varying only in the number of birds at liberty and whether they are flying or in the trees.

Not everyone agrees with the adage. Some investment brokers would rather that potential investors were prepared to take risks, while to John Bunyan, it smacked of materialism and instant gratification:

That Proverb, A Bird in the hand is worth two in the Bush, is of more Authority with them, than are all the divine testimonies of the good of the world to come. (The Pilgrim's Progress, *1678*)

In 1734 the first part of the phrase became the name of a small town in Pennsylvania, where local legend has it that two road surveyors stopped at an inn at what became the town's crossroads and decided that rather than continuing their journey in the hope of finding a wider choice of places to stay, they should remember that 'a bird in the hand, etc.' and settle where they were.

Harper's Bazaar of 23 June 1877 came up with this rejoinder:

'A bird in the hand is worth two
In the bush' – so the proverbs say;
But then, what on earth can you do,
If the bird in your hand flies away?

COLD IS THE NIGHT, WHEN THE STARS SHINE BRIGHT

When temperatures dropped in the Middle Ages, it was a serious matter. Cold could kill and fires had to be kept burning throughout the night to keep people warm. In the absence of modern forecasting equipment, telltale signs in the natural world that might indicate a particularly cold night were carefully observed. The stars were a particularly potent source of prophecy in folklore all over the world, providing a visual link to the heavens that captivated the earliest civilizations and that continues to fascinate us even in the face of our comparatively advanced modern understanding of the universe.

This particular proverb reflects the observations of seventeenth-century country-dwellers that stars appear to shine more brightly than usual when the sky is completely clear. Though unscientific, their simple rhyme was absolutely accurate. Though the stars weren't actually shining more brightly, they did appear brighter from Earth because their light was able reach the earth without being dimmed by passing through moisture in the air or being obscured from view by cloud.

Though heavy cloud cover is associated with wet and cold seasonal weather, it also serves as an insulation blanket, trapping the warm air radiating from the earth, which has been absorbing the heat of the sun during the day. In the absence of cloud the warm air dissipates and is lost into the atmosphere, leaving Earth-bound star-gazers shivering.

AN APPLE
A DAY KEEPS THE
DOCTOR AWAY

The quarterly scholarly journal *Notes and Queries* seems to have put this ancient phrase in print for the first time in 1866, describing it as a 'Pembrokeshire proverb', though the version it printed is subtly different to the one we use now:

Eat an apple on going to bed,
And you'll keep the doctor from
earning his bread.

There is evidence to suggest that the apple was held in high regard in Wales long before the health benefits we now associate them with could have begun to be understood. Several examples of early Welsh poetry are dedicated to the beauty of apple blossom, including the 'Afallennau' ('Merlin's Apple Trees') in *The Black Book of*

Camarthen, a collection of poetry which was transcribed in around 1250 but describes events from as early as the sixth century.

Another collection of early Welsh poetry, *The Red Book of Hergest*, includes descriptions of herbal remedies and makes clear the magical, curative properties of apples, describing them as a charm to combat 'all sorts of agues.'

And it seems they were right. We now know that many of the chemical properties of apples are directly beneficial to our health: they are rich in vitamin C, which reduces cholesterol and boosts the immune system; they're a rich source of phytochemicals that can act as cancer-fighting antioxidants and are believed to reduce risk of stroke, prostate cancer, Type II diabetes and asthma.

THE BEST-LAID SCHEMES O' MICE AN' MEN

This phrase is now most often used in this form to provide comfort that we're not alone when our carefully laid plans have gone wrong.

It comes from a poem called 'To a Mouse' by the Scottish poet Robert Burns, which takes the form of a regretful speech to a field mouse whose nest he has overturned while ploughing. In it he describes his sorrow for the mouse as it discovers that the home it thought it could shelter in cosily throughout the winter is no more. The verse that the proverb comes from reads:

But Mousie, thou art no thy lane
  [alone],
In proving foresight may be vain:
The best-laid schemes o' mice an' men
Gang aft agley [Often go awry],
An' lea'e us nought but grief an' pain,
For promised joy!

Burns is widely regarded as the national poet of Scotland and several of his works have become so central to the fabric of Scottish cultural life that they have woven themselves into the country's folklore. Burns also wrote the words to 'Auld Lang Syne,' which is traditionally sung on Hogmanay or New Year's Eve in Britain and the United States, while the endurance of this phrase is testament to his status as a poet. Its popularity may also have been enhanced by John Steinbeck's use of part of the phrase as the title of his 1937 novel – *Of Mice and Men*.

STILL WATERS
RUN DEEP

This phrase is thought to originate from Central Asia in the days before the Persian Empire, when the region north of the Hindu Kush was known as Bactria.

The saying is quoted in a biography of Alexander the Great, written between AD 41 and 54, by the Roman historian Quintus Curtius Rufus: 'Altissima quaeque flumina minimo sono labi,' which translates as 'The deepest rivers flow with least sound.'

As with any piece of history with such an ancient provenance, it is impossible to be sure of the details surrounding its early applications, but it seems likely that it was used literally as a reminder of the dangers of attempting to cross a river that looked calm. For Alexander the Great and his vast armies, a shallow river would have been passable but deep water was a threat. If a river ran quietly and its surface was smooth, it might be because the rocks along the riverbed were so deeply submerged that they didn't disturb the flow of water.

In 1300 the proverb appeared as 'There the flode is deppist the water standis stillist' in the popular Middle English poem *Cursor Mundi*, which is likely to have played an important role in cementing it in British folklore. The theologian Thomas Draxe included 'Where riuers runne most stilly, they are the deepest' in his *Bibliotheca scholastica instructissima. Or, Treasurie of Ancient Adagies and Sententious Proverbes* ... (1616), and it was subsequently picked up by other authors and compilers.

At some stage the saying evolved into a metaphor for the way someone with an outwardly placid temperament is often passionate or hot-blooded underneath, and this is how we use the phrase today.

A STITCH IN TIME SAVES NINE

Advocating the benefits of acting promptly, this saying simply means that fixing a problem as soon as it is spotted will save time later as it can only get worse – getting the needle and thread out to carry out a timely mend might require just a single stitch, whereas if you ignore the hole until it has grown larger you'll have to spend more time and use more stitches to mend it. ('Nine' stitches probably only because it came nearest to rhyming with 'time'.)

The phrase's literal applications would have rung true for most ordinary people in centuries gone by as fabric was very expensive and clothing had to last. Most garments were made from wool or linen and where they wore thin or tore they would have been mended.

The adage is likely to have been passed on by word of

mouth for many years before it was finally put into print in 1732 in Thomas Fuller's *Gnomologia,* in which the phrase was given, as:

A stitch in time may save nine.

In 1797 English astronomer Francis Baily left out the hesitant 'may' of Fuller's version when he noted it in his journal as 'A stitch in time saves nine', which is how we use the phrase today. It is usually employed to chivvy someone into attending to some small but irritating task that they would much rather put off indefinitely.

ST SWITHUN'S DAY IF THOU DOST RAIN

St Swithun's day if thou dost rain
For forty days it will remain.
St Swithun's day if thou be fair,
For forty days 'twill rain nae mare.

An ancient saying that blends traditional weather lore with legend. St Swithun, now sometimes written as Swithin, was a Bishop of Winchester in Saxon times who was renowned for his philanthropy and for his dedication to building churches. Legend has it that on his deathbed St Swithun asked to be buried outside, rather than in, his cathedral so that his body could, as William of Malmesbury recorded in the twelfth century, 'be subject to the feet of passers-by and to the raindrops pouring from on high.'

His last wish was granted but nine years after his death the monks of Winchester built him a shrine within the cathedral walls and moved his remains there. The legend states that during the ceremony that marked the removal of his bones, the heavens opened and there was a huge downpour, which gave rise to the piece of folklore that says St Swithun's mood on the anniversary of his removal from the fresh air determines the weather for the next forty days.

But it seems likely that the forty days part of the story came from observation of the weather patterns, as there is actually a scientific basis for this outlandish-sounding idea. In mid-July the jet stream tends to settle into position for the summer; and if by 15 July it's on a southerly pathway, bringing rain, it will often stay rainy until the end of August. If it's on a more northerly course, warmer weather will usually last.

TIME AND TIDE WAIT FOR NO MAN

This ancient phrase is often interpreted to mean that neither time nor the ebb and flow of the sea can be influenced by the actions of man, and in a broad sense, it was intended to convey the idea that mankind is powerless over nature and its unstoppable forces. But the idea that the sea was part of the image came much later as our understanding of Middle English words began to fade. An early record exists in *St Marher* (1225) which reads: 'And te tide and te time þat tu iboren were, schal beon iblescet.'

But in Middle English 'tide' meant a period of time, as in Yuletide, noontide or eventide. So in the Middle Ages the phrase meant specifically that no person was powerful enough to halt the passage of time.

The sentiment that time will keep ticking on no matter what we do appears in 'The Clerk's Tale', one of Chaucer's *Canterbury Tales*, in the lines:

For though we slepe or wake, or rome, or ryde, Ay fleeth the tyme, it nil no man abyde.

In everyday use, the phrase has become a way of encouraging someone who is taking an unnecessarily long time over something to hurry up. In the US a second line is sometimes added to the phrase to make it more useful to parents, so it ends: '. . . and the school bus waits for no boy.'

ASH BEFORE OAK

*Ash before oak the summer
is all a soak,
Oak before ash the summer
is but a splash.*

In their quest to predict what kind of fortunes they could expect in the year ahead, country folk turned to the trees for signs of how much rain the summer would bring.

Oak trees feature frequently in folklore as they were important to the Greeks, Romans, Celts and Teutonic tribes. The gods these civilizations worshipped, who had power over the fertility of the land and determined how much rain would fall, all held the oak tree as sacred, which conferred on the tree a respect that was passed down through generations of country dwellers.

The ash was also a significant tree, especially to the Druids, who believed it had healing powers, and because the oak and the ash often grow side by side in woodland, getting the same amount of sunshine and rain, they made a very convenient weather-forecasting kit. People believed that if the leaves of the ash tree unfurled before those of the oak, the summer would be rainy; if the oak came into leaf first, the summer would be mostly dry.

These days we use the snappier 'Oak before ash, in for a splash; Ash before oak, in for a soak,' though no direct correlation has been found between rainfall and the order in which these trees come into leaf. We do now know though that the oak is sensitive to temperature and its leaves unfurl as the weather gets warmer, whereas the ash is light sensitive and its leaves open as the hours of daylight lengthen. In the last ten years, as global warming has produced warmer and warmer springs, the oak has beaten the ash in seven out of ten years.

SEAGULL, SEAGULL, SIT ON THE SAND

Seagull, seagull, sit on the sand,
It's never good weather when you're on land.

In traditional fishing communities, it is unlucky to kill a seagull because they are believed to embody the souls of drowned fishermen. As 'soul birds' they are said to have prophetic powers and since medieval times those whose lives were at the mercy of the sea would take whatever guidance from them that they could. In fair weather, seagulls usually stay in flight and if they need to rest they sleep on the water. In stormy weather, they find the gusts in the air and the choppy water make it more difficult to stay at sea and often head inland. The sight of a flock of seagulls huddled together on the ground would have been worrying for the families of fishermen who were already at sea and children would recite this rhyme in the hope of bringing better weather.

These days, though, seagulls can often be found inland for a different reason: food. Though historically their diet has been small fish, they are notorious for eating almost any kind of leftovers they can lay their beaks on, and many now subsist almost entirely on the scraps they find at rubbish dumps and landfill sites, even in the finest weather.

BEGGARS CAN'T BE CHOOSERS

When this phrase first came into use in the sixteenth century, begging was a very different business to the sort we're used to today. The slow breakdown of the feudal system left many of the poorest tenant farmers dispossessed and towns and cities were inundated with poverty-stricken agricultural workers looking for food and shelter. The state did offer support for those who it determined had a valid reason for being unable to support themselves, but the rest were branded vagabonds and were looked down upon by the rest of society as idle and good for nothing.

It was against the backdrop of this hard-line attitude that this proverb became established, and when it appeared in 1546 in Heywood's *Dialogue of Proverbs*, it was recorded as:

Folke saie alwaie, beggers shulde be no choosers.

Subsequent collections usually had 'must not' – which places the emphasis firmly on the fact that beggars had no option. It meant that if a beggar was offered work or lodgings, perhaps by the Church or a privately funded charity, they should accept with good grace and be glad of whatever they were given rather than making further demands.

The first time 'Beggars *can't* be choosers' was used in print seems to be in an American novel, *Snatched from the poor-house: a young girl's life history* by N. J. Clodfelter, published in 1888. Over time, and perhaps influenced by the twentieth century's more sympathetic attitudes towards homelessness, this version has taken over, and we now most often use the phrase when describing a decision of our own to take whatever we can get if there's something we really need.

EARLY TO BED AND EARLY TO RISE

Early to bed and early to rise
Makes a man healthy, wealthy
and wise.

In the days before electricity, the hours of daylight dictated people's working patterns and this rhyme, thought to have been in use since the sixteenth century, explains the benefits of maximizing productivity by going to bed at sunset and getting up with the dawn. It first appeared in print in this form in John Clarke's collection of proverbs *Parœmiologia* in 1639, but around 1450 Dame

Juliana Berners wrote in her 'Treatise of Fishing with Angle' (published around 1496, and part of her *Boke of St Albans*):

As the olde englysshe prouerbe sayth in this wyse. Who soo woll ryse erly shall be holy helthy and zely [fortunate].

The saying was popularized in the United States by its inclusion in Benjamin Franklin's *Poor Richard's Almanack* of 1735 and remained popular in anthologies of children's rhymes throughout the eighteenth and nineteenth centuries.

Another verse, which appeared in *Little Rhymes for Little Folks* in 1812 sheds light on the attitudes towards oversleeping that prevailed at the time:

*The cock crows in the morn,
To tell us to rise,
And that he who lies late
Will never be wise:
For heavy and stupid,
He can't learn his book:
So long as he lives,
Like a Dunce he must look.*

The phrase is still used traditionally today, though its

slightly high-handed moral tone has invited modern subversions. In 1939 American satirist James Thurber wrote his own interpretation in *The New Yorker*, 'Early to rise and early to bed makes a male healthy and wealthy and dead,' which has proved almost as enduring as the original.

MAN CANNOT LIVE BY BREAD ALONE

This biblical proverb contains such an important Christian message that it appears in the Bible three times, in Deuteronomy and in the Gospels of Matthew and Luke.

The Bible story that best explains the meaning of the phrase is the Temptation of Christ described in Luke (4:3). Jesus is in the desert having fasted for forty days when the Devil comes to taunt him. He tells Jesus to use his divine power to turn the stones at his feet into loaves of bread so that he can satisfy his hunger, but though he is on the brink of starvation, Jesus replies 'It is written, Man shall not live by bread alone, but by every word that proceedeth out of the mouth of God.' The Christian interpretation of this episode is that the Gospel is what really sustains mankind and gives life value and that though the body can be sustained by food and water, to be truly alive man must follow the will of God according to the scriptures.

The phrase is still used by Christians to advocate the benefits of a modest but spiritual life, but it is also often used in more secular terms to express stoicism in the face of material hardship, implying that there are more important things in life than the trappings of wealth. Since the twentieth century the phrase has been upended and is sometimes used as a tongue-in-cheek way of justifying over-indulgence.

FROST ON THE SHORTEST DAY BODES A BAD WINTER

The winter solstice occurs on either 21 or 22 December in the northern hemisphere. It marks the day on which the sun is lowest in the sky at noon, and the hours of daylight are at their shortest. Since the twelfth century this day has been known by some Christian churches as St Thomas's day (others have it as 3 July), which features in several pieces of folklore. Celebration in these dark days was crucial to keeping up the spirits and it was traditional for farmers to make their last slaughters for the Christmas table on the shortest day, something that is illustrated by the following rhyme recorded in 1846:

The day of St Thomas, the blessed divine,
Is good for brewing, baking, and killing fat swine.

Another tradition held that the wind direction on St Thomas's day would stay the same for three months, so it was customary to look at the weathervane at midday to see what the rest of the winter would bring. If the weather was already frosty by the last week in December the rest of the winter would stay bitterly cold.

But in the Middle Ages, a 'bad' winter was actually better than a warm one. Another saying, which has now thankfully fallen out of use, warned that 'A green Christmas means a fat churchyard.' Unseasonably mild weather in December could disrupt the natural cycles of planting and growth, causing crops to fail and leaving those dependent on them for their food with nothing to live on.

WHEN THE WIND IS BLOWING IN THE NORTH

When the wind is blowing
*   in the north*
No fisherman should set forth,
When the wind is blowing
*   in the east,*
'Tis not fit for man nor beast,
When the wind is blowing
*   in the south*
It brings the food over the fish's
*   mouth,*
When the wind is blowing
*   in the west,*
That is when the fishing's best!

Or (in *The Fisherman's Magazine*):

When the wind is in the north
The skilful angler goes not forth,

When the wind is in the south
It blows the bait in the fish's mouth,
When the wind is in the east
'Tis neither fit for man nor beast,
When the wind is in the west
Then it is the very best.

In western European seas, the first version of this verse illustrates what usually happens to fishing conditions in an area of low pressure. Easterly winds, often gusty and uncomfortably warm, dry and dusty in summer and bitterly cold in winter, tend to pick up. Northerly winds around a 'low' are cold and blustery, and demand great expertise and seamanship to navigate. In contrast, southerly winds usually bring warmth, which may increase the availability of food for fish and encourage feeding behaviour useful to fishermen. The best conditions, however, come with the west wind, which tends to persist, the weather remaining fair, clear and settled. The verse conjures visions of intrepid seamen facing the hazards of Britain's famous offshore grounds: Viking, Dogger, Fisher, Wight. Yet English proverbs are as much beloved by American sportsmen who ply the waters of their continent somehow guided by the wisdom of their island-dwelling ancestors.

The verse can also apply to less hazardous, more leisurely pursuits. H. Cholmondeley-Pennell writing in *The Fisherman's Magazine and Review* in 1865 advises, 'The success of the angler greatly depends on the state of the weather. The best time to go out is after rain; do not go out when the wind is blowing from the north or from the east, as it is the worst time. A good angler will do well to bear in mind the following well-known lines . . .'

How felicitous that the best conditions for fishing are also best for a gentleman to sit beside an English stream in the peace and quiet of a long Victorian summer.

MIGHTY OAKS FROM LITTLE ACORNS GROW

The essence of this encouraging proverb can be traced back to the fourteenth century, when the idea was expressed by Chaucer in *Troilus and Criseyde* in 1374:

> *As an ook cometh of a litel spyr,*
> *So through this lettre, which that she*
> *   him sente,*
> *Encresen gan desyr, of which he*
> *   brente ...*
> *('Just as an oak comes from a little*
> *sapling, so Troilus's love [or burning*
> *desire] for Criseyde grew from the*
> *letter she had sent him.')*

Chaucer's treatment of the phrase suggests that it was used allegorically from the outset to demonstrate the way in which significant things can grow from small, insubstantial ones. Oak trees were the perfect metaphorical tool for conveying this idea because they had special status in the woodlands of Britain; they were associated with the gods of ancient civilizations and were seen as the kings of the forest, and yet every country dweller would have known from childhood that they grew from acorns small enough to fall through a hole in their pockets.

In the early 1700s Lewis Duncombe (1711–30) translated – or interpreted – the Latin tag *'De minumus maxima'* ('out of little [comes] great') as 'The lofty oak from a small acorn grows', and in 1732 the proverb appeared in Thomas Fuller's *Gnomologia* as:

> *The greatest Oaks have been little Acorns.*

In 1797 the American newspaper proprietor and poet David Everett wrote a rhyming speech to be recited by a child at a school presentation in a version closer to the one we use today:

> *Large streams from little fountains flow,*
> *Tall oaks from little acorns grow.*

Another old proverb about the oak strikes a cautionary note: 'A reed before the wind lives on, while mighty oaks do fall.' Such an event would have been observed by many – and it was the subject of one of Æsop's fables, in which a great oak is uprooted by the wind and thrown down among some reeds. It asks them how they, so light and weak, are not broken by the wind, to which they reply, 'You fight and contend with the wind, and consequently you are destroyed; while we on the contrary bend before the least breath of air, and therefore remain unbroken, and escape.'

DON'T BUY A PIG IN A POKE

It sounds an unlikely thing for anyone to do in this day and age, but the medieval marketplace was full of traders touting their livestock, and for subsistence-level farmers transporting goods in a poke (bag or sack in modern English), was often the only way they could get their wares to town. This phrase is a reference to the less scrupulous among them who would claim that their bag held a fresh suckling pig when in fact what was inside was a long way past its best, or worse still, not a pig at all. Versions of this phrase from other parts of Europe reveal that sometimes the worthless body of a dog or cat would be substituted; in French, Danish, German and Polish, the phrase translates as 'Don't buy a cat in a sack,' while in Spain the warning is even more blunt: '*Hay gato encerrado*', meaning simply 'There is a cat stuck inside.'

The phrase became a warning not to fall foul of a conman in the marketplace, and appeared in John Heywood's *Epigrammes* in 1555 as:

I will neuer bye the pyg in the poke:
Thers many a foule pyg in a feyre cloke.

Later the proverb was applied to transactions of all kinds and cautioned people to make sure they knew exactly what they were getting in return for their cash. In other words, *caveat emptor*, to use the Latin maxim – 'let the buyer beware.' These days we sometimes use the phrase retrospectively, perhaps saying that a business venture that wasn't all it was cracked up to be 'turned out to be a pig in a poke.'

THE PROOF OF
THE PUDDING IS
IN THE EATING

This seventeenth-century adage applies the wisdom of the experienced country cook to the challenges presented by life in general. It suggests that just as a pudding must be tasted before it can be declared good, any course of action can only be judged a success once it has been carried out.

It first appeared in print as 'All the proof of a pudding is in the eating,' in William Camden's *Remaines of a Greater Worke Concerning Britaine* (third edition, 1623), which was a miscellaneous collection of facts, homilies and historical titbits left over from Camden's *Britannia*, his more scholarly study of the British Isles and Ireland.

In Camden's day, of course, the 'pudding' in question would have been a more savoury affair than the sweet treats we now associate with the word. Medieval puddings were usually made by stuffing the stomach (or intestine) of a sheep or pig with suet, minced meat, oatmeal and a selection of spices, tying the ends together and boiling it. Traditionally prepared haggis is the only true pudding to have survived from the Middle Ages.

These days we sometimes use a sort of mis-abbreviated version of the phrase 'the proof is in the pudding,' which misinterprets the meaning of the word proof in the original, where it is synonymous with 'test' rather than 'evidence', as this version implies. The gist is the same as it ever was though: experience is the only way to judge anything.

A RAINBOW IN THE EASTERN SKY

A rainbow in the eastern sky, the morrow will be fine and dry. A rainbow in the west that gleams, rain tomorrow falls in streams.

Most weather lore was based on observation of the plants, animals, clouds and weathervanes that were commonplace in the lives of rural people, so the rare appearance of a rainbow, which many people interpreted as a representation of the divine, was greeted with reverence and respect. In Greek and Norse mythology the rainbow was believed to be a bridge connecting heaven and Earth, while, according to the Bible, it was a reminder of God's promise to Noah that he would never send another flood to destroy life on Earth.

Seen in these terms, the sight of a rainbow would have been comforting whatever part of the sky it appeared in, but in their endless struggle to yield a good harvest in the face of the fickle weather, medieval farmers used any sign they could to predict the weather and this method was a good one.

Rainbows are formed by sunlight refracting through droplets of water in the air and are always seen in the section of sky opposite the sun, so in the morning, as the sun rises in the east, a rainbow might appear if there were water droplets in the western sky; while in the evening, as the sun sets in the west, a rainbow in the eastern sky would signify rain clouds in the east. Since stormy weather systems move from west to east in the northern hemisphere anything we see in the west is usually heading our way, while anything in the east is usually on its way out. These days a shorter rhyme is often recited: 'Rainbow in the morning, need for a warning.'

YOU NEVER MISS A SLICE FROM A CUT LOAF

You might be forgiven for thinking that this sixteenth-century adage (sometimes rendered 'A slice off a cut loaf isn't missed') was a lesson in charitable giving – encouragement perhaps to spare some of your bread for a needy neighbour, but you'd be wrong. It is in fact, at its most savoury, a reference to petty theft, and at its least, to the perceived moral acceptability of sleeping with a woman who is already in a relationship, likening the loss of her virginity to a cut that has already been made in a loaf of bread.

It can be found in Shakespeare's first and most gruesomely violent tragedy *Titus Andronicus*, which tells the story of the fictional Roman general Titus and a terrible cycle of revenge he played out with his rival Tamora. Tamora's sons Demitrius and Chiron plot to rape Titus's daughter Lavinia, who is already promised to another man, and Demitrius justifies their plans by saying:

> *What, man! more water glideth*
>   *by the mill*
> *Than wots [knows] the miller of;*
>   *and easy it is*
> *Of a cut loaf to steal a shive [slice].*

Both John Clarke in his *Parœmiologia* (1639) and Thomas Fuller in *Gnomologia* (1732) cite the adage as it being '*safe* taking a' shive/slice 'of a cut loaf, which smacks strongly of petty criminal intent'. In Ulster the phrase 'A slice aff a cut loaf's nivver miss'd' meant that it was OK to steal something that had already been started, and the Scottish phrase 'A whang aff a new cut kebbuck [cheese] is ne'er miss'd,' was used in the same way. We also now use the phrase retrospectively when something already sub- standard has been damaged further, like when a car that's unlikely to pass its MOT takes a knock in a traffic accident.

HARES MAY PULL
DEAD LIONS BY
THE BEARD

Numerous versions of this intriguing saying exist, the earliest – 'Hares can gambol over the body of a lion' – is cited by some sources as being among the proverbs coined, or at least collected, by the Roman aphorist Publilius Syrus in his *Sententiae* in the first century BC. Other Latin versions exist – 'Even a hare will insult a dead lion,' for example – though the first record of anything similar in English is from George Pettie's 1586 translation of Stefano Guazzo's work on Italian manners, *The Civil Conversation*, which includes the lines: 'Of these this saying rose, That the lion being dead, the verie hares triumph ouer him.'

Hares are known for their timidity and this phrase was used as a way of criticizing a particular kind of cowardice that paraded as bravery. It was used against people who waited for a powerful adversary to have been fatally weakened before daring to attack them, comparing them to a hare who would flee from the slightest sound but will taunt a fearsome lion after its death.

The hare's triumph over a lion represented a worthless victory and the phrase was used to shame anyone who tried to claim bravery when their opponent, however powerful they might once have been, has lost that power. It was in this context that Shakespeare used the phrase in *King John* in 1596: 'You are the hare of whom the proverb goes, Whose valour plucks dead lions by the beard.'

BARKING DOGS SELDOM BITE

Most of us know someone who likes to sound off at full volume whenever they judge that something hasn't been done in exactly the way they would have done it. Often, these people sound fairly menacing while they're in full flow, but they're usually the least likely of our acquaintances to actually put their words into actions. In other words, their bark is worse than their bite – this contemporary-sounding saying comes from the older proverb 'Barking dogs seldom bite', which in turn has its roots in the legends of the third century.

A Middle English translation of a Greek text on the escapades of Alexander the Great called *Historia Alexandri Magni*, which became so popular in fourteenth-century Britain that Chaucer mentioned it in *The Canterbury Tales*, says this of a dog:

> *Bot as bremely [fiercely] as he baies [barks], he bitis never the faster.*

The message must have rung true with English readers

because by 1684 a more familiar version of the phrase appeared in John Bodenham's *Politeuphuia, or Wits Common-Wealth*: 'A dog that barketh much will bite little.'

Dogs were bred by the aristocracy in the seventeenth century for hunting and every nobleman kept at least one pack. Peasants couldn't afford to keep dogs as working animals or pets but semi-domesticated dogs lived alongside villagers, so the phrase's metaphorical usefulness for describing belligerent human beings would have been universally understood.

BETTER AN EGG TODAY THAN A HEN TOMORROW

This adage was first recorded in Howell's *Paramoigraphy* (Proverbs) in 1659, though it's one of the many country sayings that is likely to have been passed on by word of mouth for years prior to its appearance in print. It was used to express the view that it was better to have something for certain than to wait for something of greater value but which was not yet in your grasp. (See also 'A bird in the hand is worth two in the bush', p. 86.)

These days we often use the saying in reverse – 'Better a hen tomorrow than an egg today', a switch that relates to our relative prosperity. Though chicken appears in many recipes that have survived from the Middle Ages, it was primarily in dishes that would have been eaten by the upper classes. In more modest homes chicken was eaten rarely, while eggs were an essential ingredient of a rustic diet. Peasant families would have eaten a bird only once its laying days were definitely over; partly because in the days before artificial incubation, the odds of getting a hen from an egg probably seemed stacked against you. You needed a virile rooster; a broody mother hen who would sit for long enough for the egg's temperature to be maintained; humidity levels had to be spot on and if it did hatch, there had to be enough grain to feed the chick with. It's not hard to see why, with hungry mouths to feed, the egg today seemed a sensible option.

MISTRESS IS THE MASTER, THE PARSLEY GROWS THE FASTER

Parsley was introduced into England from Sardinia in the sixteenth century and was regarded with some suspicion as a result of its resemblance to a poisonous native plant known as fool's parsley, or dog parsley, which could be deadly if eaten.

This saying may well have referred originally to this dangerous variety of the plant, which was similar to hemlock. Wariness of the herb allowed numerous superstitions to attach themselves to it; it was considered very unlucky to give or receive a sprig of parsley as a gift. Transplanting the plant was thought to invite bad luck, or a death in the family, and if a stranger was allowed to plant parsley in the garden, whoever owned the land could expect trouble ahead.

There were also myths that related specifically to parsley's effect on women. It was said that young women who sowed its seeds would soon have a child, but that if the leaves were eaten they could prevent pregnancy. It was also said by some that, like hemlock, which was used in spells, only witches could grow it. This last belief may have been at the root of this phrase. Medieval public opinion (and indeed law) was shaped by the Church and the aristocracy, both of whom agreed that women should have few rights and be subservient to men. Women who broke this mould were often branded witches; in the Middle Ages, for the mistress to be the master of her home would have been seen as a very bad thing.

IT'S A BOLD MOUSE THAT NESTLES IN THE CAT'S EAR

Cats and mice feature frequently in folklore, providing a domestic-scale representation of the classic adversarial relationship between a hunter and its prey. In feudal times the villeins and serfs would have identified with the mice, living under the watchful eye of the lord, who was their provider but also their enemy since he had almost complete control over their lives. This saying was a warning against taking an unnecessary risk by putting themselves in close proximity to a powerful enemy. It appeared in print with this definition in George Herbert's *Outlandish Proverbs* in 1639, and served as a warning to keep your head down and do as little as possible to draw the attention of an enemy.

The phrase was given a huge boost in popularity in 1931 when it was one of the often used proverbs recited by the fictional Chinese-American detective Charlie Chan in *Charlie Chan Carries On*. The film of the book by American writer Earl Derr Biggers was a huge hit. It told of a series of murders aboard a cruise ship and included a scene in which Chan commented on the strangeness of the murderer staying on board by using the pseudo-Chinese proverb: 'Only very brave mouse makes nest in cat's ear.'

MANY THINGS GROW IN THE GARDEN THAT WERE NEVER SOWN THERE

This proverb was recorded for the first time in print in Thomas Fuller's collection of idioms *Gnomologia* (1732) as 'Many Things grow in the Garden, that were never sow'd there.' At the time, the gardens of grand, stately homes were moving away from the formal French designs that had dominated the Renaissance period towards a more natural, less cultivated style. Influential garden designers like William Kent and Lancelot 'Capability' Brown were guiding the aristocracy towards creating gardens that brought the natural world to their doors, rather than providing them with a neatly ordered refuge from it. But although this natural look was carefully planned in the grand gardens of the rich, the country gardens of the early eighteenth century were genuinely shaped by nature. Most people living in the countryside grew vegetables in small kitchen gardens, but in the days before chemical weed killer, countless unplanned plants would have sprung up every year. Weeds like shepherd's purse, fat hen or goosefoot, cleaver, speedwell and hairy bittercress all disperse their seeds by wind, which meant that they could spread from uncultivated land into gardens on the breeze.

But country gardeners wouldn't have expected otherwise and this understanding that unplanned plants would appear in their gardens taught them to expect the unexpected, which is the broader meaning of this phrase.

WHEN POVERTY COMES IN AT THE DOOR, LOVE FLIES OUT OF THE WINDOW

This mercenary message has its origins in medieval marriage, when love was rarely the driving force behind a match. A similar idea is described in William Caxton's 1474 translation of a thirteenth-century Italian political treatise, which used chess pieces as an allegory for a society. Caxton's version says:

> *Herof men saye a comyn prouerbe in englond that loue lasteth as longe as the money endurith.*

The proverb seems to have referred to relationships between members of the upper classes, where there was money to endure. While little was done to hide the fact it was business, rather than mutual affection, that determined who married whom, the twelfth century had seen the birth of the notion of courtly love, which although unlinked to marriage, did introduce the idea of love as something to be aspired to.

The exact phrase is described as an old maxim in *The English Gentlewoman*, by wealthy country gent Richard Brathwaite, published in 1631, which advised respectable women on how to behave. In this case it required them to guard against allowing this proverb to prove true if their own husbands lost their fortunes, in which circumstances the ladylike thing would be to honour and obey him regardless.

Nowadays the phrase is somewhat outdated, but it is still occasionally used by members of the older generations to warn youngsters against getting married before they've established themselves with a way of earning a living, or as an arch way of passing judgement on celebrity couples whose relationships come to an end the moment one of their stars begins to fade.

TOO MANY COOKS
SPOIL THE BROTH

Cooks were the head of the kitchen in the Middle Ages and were often great sources of folklore as they were respected in the community and had usually served long apprenticeships learning their skills. This proverb makes the point that incorporating the ideas of too many people, especially people who are used to being in charge of their own domain, tends not to have an end result that represents the sum of their skills, but rather one that is much less successful than what they could have achieved on their own.

The adage can be traced back to the late sixteenth century, when it was more often given as 'the more cooks, the worse potage', potage being a kind of thick, stew-like soup made from oats that was common in medieval cooking.

Broth or potage is excellent for making the point of the proverb because of the individual preferences of each cook for how much seasoning to add and which additional ingredients to use. Potage was usually made from whatever could be had from the kitchen garden: leeks, turnips or carrots made a simple background flavour, but herbs, spices and plenty of salt were added to make it taste good – ingredients that work well in the right quantities but which could make the dish completely unpalatable if the balance was wrong.

Still popular today, the phrase is often abbreviated to 'Too many cooks . . .' and used in work environments when too many people wanting to have their say on a particular project threatens the quality of what they produce. In 1979, *The Guardian* commented:

It was a great mistake to think that administration was improved by taking on more administrators ... 'Too many cooks spoil the broth.'

TAKE THE BIT BETWEEN YOUR TEETH

This saying has been in use since the seventeenth century to spur people into taking control of a situation by evoking the image of a horse taking control back from his rider. The bit is the mouthpiece that allows the pressure being put on a horse's reins to be felt in the softest part of a horse's mouth, which means that it is forced to turn its head in the direction its rider wants to go. A horse taking the bit between its teeth, rather than allowing it to pull at the more sensitive skin, was a gesture of defiance in a young horse that hadn't been broken in. Metaphorically, the saying serves as an encouragement to wrest back control of a situation from whoever has been forcing you along a certain path so that you can follow the direction you choose for yourself.

The earliest record of the phrase in print can be found in John Dryden's satirical poem *The Medal*, published in 1682:

> *But this new Jehu spurs*
>   *the hot-mounted horse,*
> *Instructs the beast to know*
>   *his native force,*
> *To take the bit between*
>   *his teeth and fly*
> *To the next headlong steep*
>   *of anarchy . . .*

The saying is still used to encourage people to take control of the direction of their lives by tapping into their innate strength, though these days the bite-sized proverb has been largely replaced by a libraries' worth of self-help books that each take hundreds of pages to make the same point.

SOMETHING OLD, SOMETHING NEW

Something old, something new,
Something borrowed, something blue.

Weddings are among the ceremonies to which we still attach the most folklore. Rituals which have long been abandoned in other arenas of our lives seem suddenly crucial on our wedding days, as though for one day only we're willing to do everything within our power to make sure our marriages aren't jinxed. It's superstition that drives it; this saying, which is thought to be Victorian in origin, dictates that a bride must wear or carry something old, something new, something borrowed, something blue with her up the aisle as good-luck charms. Traditionally, a woman's wedding dress would have been old, handed down from one generation to the next and altered each time to fit. These days the dress is most likely to be the new item on the list, with a piece of family jewellery serving as something borrowed, and perhaps old as well.

The addition of something blue may be connected to the Roman custom of dressing brides in blue to symbolize love and purity. Until the nineteenth century it was common for English brides to wear blue rather than white, reflecting the attire of the Virgin Mary to emphasize their modesty. Another rhyme from the Victorian era that reflects this tradition goes: 'Marry in blue, lover be true.'

In the original version of the rhyme there is a final line that we tend to omit today: 'And a silver sixpence in her shoe.' The tradition of a lucky sixpence representing financial security still has a place in today's wedding customs –though it's more likely to be found decorating the wedding cake than in the bride's shoe.

DON'T GO NEAR THE WATER UNTIL YOU'VE LEARNT TO SWIM

This caution against impatience has been in use since the early nineteenth century, when swimming began to become a popular pastime. Although swimming had been enjoyed by early civilizations, and pools specifically for swimming, rather than simply bathing, were built by the Romans, it fell out of favour in the Middle Ages because of the fear of infection and the role water might play in the spread of disease.

Even though people in cities blithely drank water from rivers that were also a repository for sewage and other noxious waste, they distrusted the idea of being completely submerged in water. Those who did swim in this era usually used a form of breast stroke that allowed the head to be held high out of the water to avoid contaminated liquid entering their bodies through the ear. This meant that it wasn't just a fear of drowning that made parents warn their children about staying away from the water until they could swim, they also had to have mastered a stroke which, they hoped, would prevent them from catching anything.

The phrase appeared in H. G. Bohn's *Handbook of Proverbs* in 1855, from which time at least it has served as a warning against putting yourself in any situation that might be dangerous until you are certain you know how to handle it. Other phrases serve a similar purpose, and in the UK we now tend to prefer 'Don't try to run before you can walk.'

STY, STY, LEAVE MY EYE

Sty, sty, leave my eye
Take the next one coming by.

This ancient remedy for a sty in the eye comes straight from the spell books of medieval wise women. In the Middle Ages few country people could afford to visit an apothecary and, in any case, in the days before antibiotics there was little that could have been done to help cure a sty, which is caused by a bacterial infection. Left to its own devices in the days when the concept of hygiene was unknown, it could have taken several weeks to heal.

Wise women were the first port of call for people seeking relief from a huge range of maladies – they were experts in the blending of plants and herbs to make cures and many of their remedies were effective because of the medicinal properties in the plants.

A spell was often used in conjunction with an ointment or potion. In the case of sties, there were various techniques that could be used while reciting an incantation. Some methods suggested rubbing the tail of a black cat over the affected eye nine times, others say a stolen dishcloth should be wiped over the eye and then secretly buried, but if you were serious about getting rid of your sty you had to walk backwards to the crossroads, spit on the ground three times over your right shoulder and then deliver the line 'Sty, sty, leave my eye; take the next one coming by', so that the next person to arrive at the crossroads would take your sty from you.

LIGHTNING NEVER STRIKES TWICE

This mid-nineteenth-century maxim is used as an assurance in difficult times that once you've experienced misfortune, the same kind of difficulty will never befall you again. It's a rare example of a piece of folklore in which the wisdom about the natural world employed to make the wider point is actually flawed. There is no evidence to suggest that once something, or even someone, has been struck by lightning once they won't be struck again. In fact, there is plenty of proof of the contrary. American park ranger Roy Sullivan was struck a record seven times between 1942 and 1977 and made it into the *Guinness Book of Records*. Many tall buildings are struck countless times, which is why the tallest building in an area usually has a lightning conductor on its roof to ground the lightning bolt to prevent it from damaging the structure.

The reason for this mistaken belief may have its roots in rural communities in the days when buildings were much lower and wouldn't have been struck at all. The most common feature of the early nineteenth-century landscape to absorb a lightning strike would have been trees. And when trees are struck by lightning they usually burn down, which meant that by the time the next electrical storm occurred, they were no longer the tallest structure in the area and wouldn't be struck again.

We still use the phrase today to comfort people getting over an unpleasant experience, by reassuring them that they are in some way immune from the same bad luck.

COLD HANDS, WARM HEART

This saying is thought to have entered English folklore through the French phrase *'froides mains, chaudes amours'*, collected in Georges de Backer's *Dictionnaire des Proverbes François* (1710).

An early record of the saying in the English language can be found in V. S. Lean's *Collectanea*, a collection of superstitions and folklore published in 1903, so it is likely that it was in regular use from at least the latter half of the nineteenth century.

It has also been used traditionally as a playful way of judging whether someone is in love, cold hands being a sure sign that they are. This latter usage has its origins in palmistry, in which a lack of blood flow in the hands is said to indicate that all the warm blood is flowing through the heart, which is the principal organ of passion. While the link between love and poor circulation does not have a foundation in science, there is a biological basis for the phrase. When exposed to low temperatures or emotional stress that might signify some other source of danger, the body does respond by concentrating the blood flow to the vital organs, which keeps them warm while allowing the less crucial extremities to lose heat until the threat has passed. In the most literal sense then, those with cold hands probably do have a warm heart.

On the other hand, recent scientific research has shown that when a person's hands are warm, he or she is likely to feel warmer and more generous towards other people. Even so, we still often use the saying as a cheering rejoinder if someone finds our hands cold, but it is most frequently applied to people who seem icy but are warm-hearted or passionate beneath their cool exterior. (See also 'Still waters run deep', p.93.)

A WATCHED POT
NEVER BOILS

While this old proverb clearly has no truth in it, it is a powerful illustration of the way our perception of time passing is affected by the attention we pay it. It is likely to have been in use for years prior to its first appearance in print in Victorian novelist Elizabeth Gaskell's 'Tale of Manchester Life', *Mary Barton*, in 1848.

In the book the phrase is used by a kindly fisherman's wife whose language is peppered with proverbs. She says it to discourage Mary from sitting up all night watching for the arrival of a witness who can prove that the man she loves is innocent of murder. The stakes couldn't be higher and the example demonstrates the way the phrase seems at its most true when whatever you're waiting for really matters.

Those who first used the saying would have had in mind a cast-iron pot containing water or stew, which if you were hungry or in a hurry might have seemed to take for ever to boil on the stove or over an open fire. Electricity has made most kitchen processes much quicker, but we understand the frustrations of longing for things to happen over which we have no control just as well as people did in Gaskell's day, and the phrase is still used to encourage people to find something else to do to take their mind off whatever it is they're waiting for, so that the time will seem to pass more quickly.

WHEN CLOUDS APPEAR LIKE ROCKS AND TOWERS

When clouds appear like rocks
and towers,
The earth will be washed
by frequent showers.

One of the most reliable methods farmers and sailors had for making accurate weather forecasts before the arrival of modern technology was cloud watching. It wouldn't have allowed them to make long-term predictions, but it could often give a clear idea of what the weather would be like later that day and into the next.

The clouds in this old rhyme match the description of what we now refer to as cumulonimbus clouds – dense, rock-like clouds that can measure several miles across. Strong updraughts cause these clouds to form vertically, building up like towers into middle altitudes where their tops are sheared off by fast horizontal winds. These flat tops have led them to be given the nickname 'anvil clouds'. Their name is a blend of two Latin words, *cumulus*, meaning accumulated and *nimbus*, meaning rain.

Unlike many pieces of weather lore, which were used by farmers, fishermen or sailors, this one makes specific mention of the earth, rather than the sea. This is because cumulonimbus usually form over land as a result of the change in pressure caused by the heat escaping from the earth in the afternoon after it has absorbed the sun's heat during the day.

These clouds are responsible for sudden downpours and they often produce wind and lightning, but because they form where the air pressure is unstable and changeable, they are not associated with steady rain and their impact is short-lived.

IF WISHES WERE HORSES, THEN BEGGARS WOULD RIDE

This sixteenth-century proverb stresses that wishing for something you want is useless, for so many wishes are made that if each was a horse, there would be enough horses for even the lowliest of beggars to ride. It is also interpreted as a lesson that wishes don't come true because if they did, each man would already have had his wishes granted and beggars would be elevated to a status that would allow them the luxury of a horse.

The sentiment was recorded with a different metaphorical image in 1605 in William Camden's collection of facts and adages, *Remaines of a Greater Worke,*

Concerning Britaine. His version went: 'If wishes were thrushes beggers would eat birds'. Horses had entered the equation by 1670, when John Ray's *Collection of English Proverbs* included a pleasingly rhyming version: 'If wishes would bide, beggers would ride', and at some point in the sixteenth century a longer verse was devised and set to music to form a nursery rhyme that went:

If wishes were horses
Beggars would ride;
If turnips were watches
I would wear one by my side.
And if 'ifs' and 'ands'
Were pots and pans,
The tinker would never work!

The phrase is still regularly used today to admonish people for wasting time longing for things rather than taking whatever action they can to make them happen. It's generally abbreviated to 'If wishes were horses . . .' and delivered with a wagging finger or an arched brow.

APRIL SHOWERS BRING MAY FLOWERS

This piece of ancient weather lore dates back to the mid-sixteenth century and refers in a literal sense to the benefits of the repeated rain showers characteristic of April for successful plant growth the following month.

It featured in a long poem by the musician, poet and farmer Thomas Tusser in *A Hundreth Good Pointes of Husbandrie* (published in 1557, to be expanded to *Five Hundreth Pointes of Good Husbandrie* in 1573) in the form of the couplet:

> *Sweet April showers*
> *Do spring May flowers.*

Showers of the sort we expect in April are the result of the start of the warmer season. The sun heats the earth all morning and as the heat rises from the ground into the air during the afternoon, the air becomes less dense and begins to rise. As it rises it cools and the water vapour in the air condenses and forms clouds. As temperatures rise towards mid-afternoon, these clouds reach their maximum height and the water falls as rain. But the showers only last as long as the rising temperatures and as the air cools with the approach of evening, the skies usually clear, creating a pattern of showers that delivers the optimum dose of water to flowers preparing to come into bloom.

In later years the phrase has come to be used to encourage optimism, as a metaphor for the notion that the experience of something unpleasant, represented here by rain, is often followed by something good.

THE EARLY BIRD CATCHES THE WORM

Just as the first robin or thrush to rise will beat his feathered friends to the juiciest worm, so those who rise (or arrive at their place of work) early will triumph over their competitors (see also 'Early to bed and early to rise,' p. 102). This reliable old adage, which takes its lesson from the natural world, was recorded in William Camden's *Remaines Concerning Britaine* (fifth edition 1736) and in John Ray's *Collection of English Proverbs* in 1670 as:

The early bird catcheth the worm.

It has remained in such regular use that from it we have taken the term 'early bird' to mean someone who habitually gets up early in the morning. We also use 'early bird' in a commercial setting to describe holidaymakers who make early bookings to secure the cheapest deals, and to diners who eat early in the evening and can therefore order from a cheaper, 'early bird' menu.

In very recent use calling someone an 'early bird' in a work setting has come to have negative connotations, suggesting that they're overly keen to get an advantage over their colleagues or eager to please the boss at the expense of their fellow employees.

At some point in the twentieth century a humorous rejoinder came into use: 'The early bird catches the worm, but the second mouse gets the cheese.'

PUTTING THE CART BEFORE THE HORSE

This ancient saying is used to suggest that someone has done something the wrong way round and makes its point by example. Putting the cart in front of the horse rather than behind would make it impossible for the horse to pull the cart along as is intended. It's a nonsensical reversal of a correct sequence with the purpose of demonstrating the importance of maintaining the proper order of things.

The Roman philosopher and orator Cicero used the phrase (along with another well-known one) in his work *On Friendship*, written in around 44 BC, by which time the saying was already well established:

> *We suffer from carelessness in many of our undertakings: in none more than in selecting and cultivating our friends. We put the cart before the horse, and shut the stable door when the steed is stolen, in defiance of the old proverb.*

It was first recorded in English in 1589 in George Puttenham's *The arte of English poesie,* an authoritative treatise on the art and history of poetry which included a section on figures of speech. Puttenham wrote:

> *We call it in English prouerbe, the cart before the horse, the Greeks call it* Histeron proteron.

Histeron proteron translates as 'latter before' and was a Greek figure of speech used to describe the literary device of switching the order of words to emphasize the most important ones. Outside the realm of literature, the phrase was usually employed as a warning not to do things the wrong way round and this is how the phrase is most commonly used today. By extension it has also come to be used as a caution against trying to do something before you have properly prepared (see also 'Don't go near the water until you've learnt to swim', p. 131.)

TROUT JUMP HIGH WHEN A RAIN IS NIGH

This old nugget of fisherman's lore is a prime example of cause and effect in the natural world. The country folk who first used the sight of leaping fish as a way of foretelling showers can have had no idea of the atmospheric changes that caused the phenomenon, but it didn't matter why the fish did it, what mattered was that when they did it, it really did signal rain.

Alterations in atmospheric pressure are one of the best predictors of changes in the weather because weather arrives in bands of high and low pressure. The first mercury barometer, an instrument we still use today to monitor changes in pressure, was invented by Italian physicist Evangelista Torricelli in 1643, but the device wasn't found in people's homes until the following century, so people looked for other signs that air pressure was changing.

A drop in atmospheric pressure means the air is rising away from the earth at a faster rate than air from the surrounding areas can flow in to replace it. In these conditions, even gases trapped under water, say those produced by rotting plant life on the bottom of a lake or pond, begin to rise, bubbling up to the surface and taking with them a feast of microscopic organisms from the nutrient-rich depths. Small fish that feed on these organisms race to the surface in pursuit of these bubbles and the bigger fish are hot on their trail, often leaping into the air in a feeding frenzy.

CURSES, LIKE CHICKENS, COME HOME TO ROOST

This medieval version of our modern saying 'what goes around comes around' has its origins in fourteenth-century notions of morality. Chaucer gave expression to the idea at the end of the fourteenth century in 'The Parson's Tale', with the line:

And ofte tyme swiche cursynge wrongfully retorneth agayn to hym that curseth, as a bryd that retorneth agayn to his owene nest.

Cursing in this context meant wishing ill on others, so Chaucer's suggestion was that whatever ill fortune a man might wish on someone else would eventually befall the man himself.

Chickens seem to have replaced the more generic 'bryd' of the original some time in the eighteenth century, when hens were kept by most households and their habit of roaming freely during the day but returning to their own coop for the night would have been familiar to most early users of the phrase. It finally appeared in print in the modern form on the title page of the Romantic poet Robert Southey's epic poem *The Curse of Kehama*, in which an evil priest puts a curse on a man for killing his son but is ultimately defeated by the man, who has grown in strength as a result of the curse.

The proverb has been so well used over the years that the part about curses has worn away. We now say simply 'the chickens have come home to roost,' when we find ourselves facing the consequences of any kind of past bad behaviour.

WHEN BEES TO DISTANCE WING THEIR FLIGHT

Bees have fascinated mankind for centuries, and a belief that they can predict rain dates back to the ancient Greeks, who were the first to practise beekeeping. They noticed that bees stayed close to the hive when a storm was imminent and flew further afield on clear days. North African folklore also featured bees as weather forecasters; there people believed the tone and pitch of their hum foretold whether the day would be wet or dry.

The behaviour of insects was often studied carefully for hints about alterations in the weather and we now know that the drop in atmospheric pressure that precedes a storm is the trigger for the changes that can be observed in flying insects. Low air pressure makes it more difficult for both birds and insects to fly, so they tend to fly closer to the ground before a storm (see also 'If birds fly low, then rain we shall know', p. 77). Bees have an added incentive to stay close to home if heavy rain threatens because they are likely to perish in a downpour, so while beekeepers often observe bees flying out in light drizzle, which is actually beneficial for the collection of nectar, they rarely see them going far if there are heavy clouds. Modern science had an additional theory about this – that bees need some clear sky to help them navigate on long journeys. In cloudy conditions it is suggested that they have a much poorer chance of finding their way home.

IT'S ALL GRIST TO THE MILL

This commonly used saying originates in the flour mills of medieval England. It has been in use since at least the sixteenth century, when a similar phrase 'bring grist to the mill' was used idiomatically to mean to turn something to your advantage. The original wording of the proverb was 'All is grist that comes to the mill' and the phrase had faintly negative undertones, suggesting that someone was taking advantage, perhaps as a result of its roots in feudal society.

In early medieval England, each family took their grain (known as grist) to be ground at a communal mill attached to each manor. The miller was employed by the lord and charged a fee for grinding the villagers' grain. Money was scarce so this usually took the form of a share of the grain, which in lean years would have cost a poor family dearly. In this way a miller could make a profit for the lord of the manor at the expense of the peasants, with whatever grain came to the mill, regardless of its quality.

The phrase was used metaphorically from the outset to show that all experience, both good and bad, can be useful. Over time, the positive aspects of this have largely superseded its links to feudal injustice and it now often means simply that every little helps. However, it is sometimes used to describe factors that seem to add weight to an opponent's argument even though we might believe those factors to be worthless.

SEPARATE THE SHEEP FROM THE GOATS

This saying comes from the Gospel of Matthew and appeared in Middle English for the first time in the earliest complete printed English translation of the Bible, that of Myles Coverdale in 1535. It is taken from the parable of the sheep and the goats, which is often interpreted as a depiction of what will happen on Judgement Day. In the King James Bible, the section from which the phrase comes (Matthew 25:32–3) reads:

> *And before him shall be gathered all nations: and he shall separate them one from another, as a shepherd divideth his sheep from the goats: And he shall set the sheep on his right hand, but the goats on the left.*

In Christian minds, sheep were associated with meekness and goodness, congregations were often referred to as a flock, Jesus was known as the Lamb of God and also as the Good Shepherd. Goats, meanwhile, were giddy and fickle, with eyes and horns like the Devil's.

The parable goes on to explain how the 'sheep', who

are righteous in the eyes of the Lord because they have shown kindness and charity towards the sick and needy, personified by Jesus, will be welcomed into heaven, while the goats, who have failed to help Jesus, will be cast into hell.

The phrase retained a strictly religious meaning until the nineteenth century, when it began to be used more broadly to describe other opposites in quality. Now we use it in the workplace when we think a certain challenge will sort those who take part into high and low performers. Other versions of the phrase have also developed, such as 'Separate the wheat from the chaff' and the more recent marketing slogan for a flu remedy: 'Sorts the men from the boys.'

IF THE COCK GOES CROWING TO BED

If the cock goes crowing to bed,
He'll certainly rise with a watery
head.

The farmyard cockerel makes his presence known every morning when he crows to herald the dawn, and his forceful cry has earned him a place at the heart of English folklore. He was credited with the magical ability to scare off the spirits of darkness with his call, leaving the farmer and his family safe to get up when they heard it. West Country wisdom said that the cockerel could frighten away even the Devil himself, while in Celtic and Welsh mythology a cockerel crowing three times around midnight was believed to foretell a death.

The idea that an evening rendition of cock-a-doodle-doo would mean the bird would wake up wet comes from the belief, prevalent in rural communities, that a cock crowing in the evening signalled that there would be rain by the morning. While cockerels usually reserve their call for first light, they do also crow if there's a disturbance near by and if they sense that rain is on the way. While traditional beliefs state that the cockerel's premonition of rain was linked to its magical powers, we now know that birds are particularly sensitive to changes in air pressure, and that cockerels crow when atmospheric pressure drops in advance of a rain storm, either as an expression of discomfort at the change or as a warning to its hens to gather together to shelter from the forthcoming showers.

A SWARM OF BEES
IN MAY IS WORTH A
LOAD OF HAY

The ancient Egyptians were the first to discover the delights of honey and records of beekeeping date the practice back to 13,000 BC. In medieval England honey was the main source of sweetness in cooking and was believed to have magical healing powers derived from the flowers whose nectar was used to make it. In rural communities it was thought to cure everything from digestive problems to coughs and colds, and it was even taken to counter the effects of opium and was used to embalm bodies, so it was one of the most valuable commodities of the time.

Unlike today's beekeepers, peasants in the Middle Ages collected their honey from natural hives, which they often transferred into homemade beehives called skeps made from coiled and woven straw. These containers couldn't be opened and closed again as modern containers can, so when the time came for collecting the honey in September the hive was destroyed and the bees died. Every year the beekeeper would have to find a new swarm; if he was lucky and found one, he'd have enough honey to last the year, which, as this sixteenth-century proverb shows, was at least equal in worth to his hay harvest.

But the window of opportunity for settling a new swarm was short, as the full verse explains:

A swarm of bees in May
Is worth a load of hay;
A swarm of bees in June
Is worth a silver spoon;
A swarm of bees in July
Is not worth a fly.

CUT YOUR COAT ACCORDING TO YOUR CLOTH

This instructive saying has been used since the sixteenth century to encourage people to live within their means, and was already listed as a proverb in John Heywood's 1546 collection of proverbs. It refers specifically to the cutting of fabric by tailors or housewives, and some interpretations of the phrase take it as a straightforward example of limiting yourself to what you have at your disposal.

Others cite another possible source: the strict laws that governed who wore what in Elizabethan England. In around 1574 Elizabeth I passed several 'sumptuary' laws (named after the Latin word for expenditure) called 'statutes of apparel', which dictated with astonishing detail the colours, cuts and fabrics that could be worn by people of each social class. Laws preventing overspending on frivolities, food and entertainment had been a feature of Roman courts and in Tudor times they were justified as a means of preventing people from getting into debt, but the rules were as much about emphasizing class divisions as they were about protecting the well-to-do from overspending.

They decreed that purple must only be worn by royalty and that silk be reserved for only those of knightly status or above, while lower-class women must limit themselves to wool, linen or sheepskin in orange, beige or yellow.

The cloth you cut your coat from might therefore have been determined not only by what you could afford, but by what your social status allowed you, so the phrase was a reminder to know your place as well as to spend only what you could afford. These days the snob factor is absent from the phrase's meaning but we still use it to warn big spenders against overloading the credit card.

NEEDS MUST WHEN THE DEVIL DRIVES

Society in the Middle Ages was religious in a way that is difficult to grasp in our secular age. Right and wrong were determined by the Bible, thanks were given to God for good fortune and whenever anything bad happened it was attributed to the Devil. Hell was a very real and terrifying place in medieval minds and it was against demonic forces, rather than plain old adversity, that people battled on a daily basis. It was also widely recognized that poverty made people vulnerable to the influence of the Devil, who was always looking for signs of weakness that he could capitalize on in his efforts to turn man away from God. The ever-present threat he posed means that the Devil looms large in English folklore.

The original wording of this saying appears in John Lydgate's *The Assembly of the Gods*, published around 1420: 'Hit ys oft seyde by hem that yet lyues, He must nedys go that the deuell dryues.'

In this form the phrase uses the familiarity of a harnessed animal being driven onwards to convey the impossibility of man resisting the Devil when he has the reins. Over the centuries the phrase has been gradually shortened so that the version we use today makes no mention of the Devil at all. 'Needs must,' we sigh as we're grudgingly forced by circumstance to do something we'd rather avoid.

YOU CAN'T TEACH
AN OLD DOG
NEW TRICKS

When it first appeared in print in John Fitzherbert's *Boke of Husbandry* in 1523, this old adage seems to have been meant literally. 'The dogge must lerne it when he is a whelpe, or els it wyl not be; for it is harde to make an olde dogge to stoupe,' he explained.

But as with so many long-lasting pieces of farming wisdom, what started out as a simple observation of animal behaviour soon became adopted as a more broadly applicable piece of folklore. It was certainly being used figuratively by 1546, when habitual gatherer of proverbs John Heywood bagged it for his collection and spelt out its meaning as an expression of the impossibility of getting an elderly person to change their ways.

In those days dogs were strictly working animals in rural communities and few farmers would have had time for teaching tricks. It wasn't until the late seventeenth century that the 'new tricks' became part of the phrase, but once established, the wording stuck as we still use it in exactly this form today. Nowadays, though, it is most often used by the elderly themselves as a way of discouraging enthusiastic youngsters from trying to educate them in the use of modern technology which they have no desire to use.

LOOK BEFORE YOU LEAP

This familiar warning against acting without thinking is thought to have its roots in Æsop's fable 'The Fox and the Goat', written in the fifth century BC. In the Middle Ages, when the phrase began to be used on its own as a proverb, the influence of Æsop on the moral conscience of the population was enormous. His fables were read and recited repeatedly, images from them were depicted on tapestries, carvings and sculptures and they even found their way into Christian and Catholic sermons, so it was a small step for the lessons they contained to become part of the rich body of folklore that guided so much of everyday life.

In the story that gave rise to this phrase a fox falls into a well and can't get out. When a goat passes the well and asks the fox if the water is sweet, the fox describes how delicious it is and persuades the goat to come in and taste it. The goat takes the fox's recommendation at face value and without thinking about the fact that he won't be able to get out either, joins him in the well. The fox then tells the goat to let him climb on his back to get out of the well, promising to pull the goat up after him. The goat again complies, only for the fox to run off as soon as he is free, leaving the goat to languish at the bottom of the well.

The maxim appeared in an early manuscript dating back to around 1350 (Douce MS 52 no. 150) as 'First loke and aftirward lepe'. And it is cited in *Obedience of Christian Man* (1528) by the first person to translate the Bible into

English for a lay readership, William Tyndale: 'We say …
Loke yer thou lepe, whose literall sence is, doo nothinge
sodenly or without avisement.'

It was also associated from very early in its usage with
that most momentous and un-take-backable of decisions:
whom to marry. It appeared in John Heywood's *Dialogue
of Proverbs* of 1546 with the following verse:

> *And though they seeme wives
>   for you never so fit,
> Yet let not harmfull haste so
>   far out run your wit:
> But that ye harke to heare
>   all the whole summe
> That may please or displease
>   you in time to cumme.
> Thus by these lessons ye may
>   learne good cheape
> In wedding and all things to
>   looke ere ye leaped.*

Though this rhyme seems to have been forgotten, we
still use the saying, delivered with a cautionary tone, to
remind friends not to make hasty decisions that they
won't be able to take back.

WHAT IS SAUCE FOR THE GOOSE IS SAUCE FOR THE GANDER

In the Middle Ages, goose was as popular as chicken at the tables of the upper classes. Even those who couldn't afford the luxury of meat with every meal would eat the bird on special occasions, especially at Michaelmas and Whitsuntide. Little distinction was made in the medieval kitchen between the female goose and the male gander; both were roasted and were traditionally served with a sauce made either from dark prunes or cooked garlic.

The phrase seems to have been used figuratively from the start to convey the idea that what is adequate for one person should be adequate for another and, more explicitly, that what's good enough for the woman of the household should be good enough for the man. An earlier saying expounding this message was recorded in John Heywood's *Dialogue of Proverbs* as 'As well for the coowe calf as for the bull,' and by the time John Ray listed it in his collection of proverbs in 1670, it appeared with the explanatory note: 'This is a woman's proverb.' Perhaps what he meant by this was that it was a proverb most likely to be used by women as they tried to persuade their husbands that being the man of the house didn't mean they deserved any kind of special treatment.

These days we abbreviate the phrase to 'What's sauce for the goose' and use it most often to express the need for equality.

DON'T SPOIL THE SHIP FOR A HA'PORTH OF TAR

Nautical wisdom features widely in folklore and as a consequence it has been mistakenly cited as the source of a number of proverbs which actually have their roots in the soil rather than the sea. This saying, which warns against risking something precious for the sake of a small additional investment, is one of them.

Since ships could quite conceivably be spoiled through scrimping on the tar used to seal their hulls, a naval origin is very plausible. But this phrase actually comes from farming, not sailing. Before chemical disinfectants became available to farmers they used tar to seal wounds on their livestock (pigs, sheep, cattle) to prevent them from becoming infected. Try saying 'sheep' in the sort of accent a rural Elizabethan peasant might have had and you'll see how the confusion arose. John Ray's *Collection of English Proverbs* (1670) featured the original:

Ne'er lose a hog for a half-penny-worth of tarre.

To which Ray added the comment: 'Some have it, lose not a sheep. Indeed, tarre is more used about sheep than swine.'

The phrase is still used to appeal to people not to risk the failure of an enterprise for the sake of a small piece of additional investment, but also in the broader context of human endeavour, to encourage people not to risk sacrificing a sensitive political deal or the resolution of a family feud for the sake of petty details.

IT'S NO USE CRYING
OVER SPILT MILK

When this still well-used proverb was first uttered the milk it referred to probably came from goats or sheep as cows' milk only became commonplace towards the end of the sixteenth century. Demand for milk was high because it was needed for making medieval essentials such as butter and cheese, but milking was done by hand and yielded small amounts compared to today's industrialized milking machines. This made the product a precious commodity and one you might well have felt the urge to shed a tear over if you or the goat you were milking had been the one to overturn the milk pail.

In 1659, James Howell in his collection of proverbs, *Paramoigraphy*, recorded the saying as 'No weeping for shed milk,' which was put to use outside the milking shed to encourage people not to be unhappy about what couldn't be undone. The idea that it wasn't worth getting upset over things for which there was no remedy had been set out as early as 1484 in William Caxton's translation of *Æsop's Fables*. He described as a doctrine the instruction to 'take no sorowe of the thynge lost whiche may not be recouered.'

Now, with the price of milk well within the means of most pockets, we often misinterpret the phrase and assume that the spilt milk in the proverb represents something of little value. With this idea in mind we tend to use the phrase when someone seems unduly upset over some small matter that really doesn't warrant losing sleep over, rather than over some mishap, possibly serious, that cannot be undone.

THERE'S MANY A SLIP BETWEEN CUP AND LIP

This warning against celebrating a victory before you are certain of it was being used in English by at least 1539, when it appeared in Richard Taverner's translation of the proverbs of Erasmus as 'Many thynges fall betwene the cuppe and the mouth.' As this link with the famous Dutch scholar of Latin suggests, it found its way into English folklore from the mythology of Ancient Greece. Greek legend has it that the lesson in the proverb was learnt the hard way by a man who scoffed at a prophecy that he wouldn't live to drink the wine that came from his own vineyard. Having successfully tended his vines, harvested his grapes and produced his wine, he was about to sip from his glass and prove the prophecy false when he learnt that a wild boar was running amok in his vineyard. So he set down his glass and ran outside to chase the boar off, only for the animal to turn its attentions to him and gore him to death.

While it's hard to imagine anything so dramatic occurring once you've got a wine glass in your hand in modern life, the metaphor is useful in certain business situations that shouldn't be taken for granted until the final signature has been added (see also 'Don't count your chickens before they've hatched,' p.78), and is certainly applicable in all matters relating to house buying.

CROOKED LOGS MAKE STRAIGHT FIRES

The earliest mention of this phrase in print came in Randle Cotgrave's English-French dictionary published in 1611. Alongside the 50,000 word definitions his book featured around 1,500 proverbs, which provide a fascinating picture of the sayings in use at the time. Few are still recognizable today but this one is still used to warn against judging people by their outward appearance.

The phrase was probably in use for several decades, if

not centuries, before Cotgrave recorded it, as the matter of how to build a good fire had been of great significance to man before the English language was even dreamt of. As with many pieces of country folklore, the saying came from observation of the way things worked rather than an understanding of why they worked, but we now know that the phrase is true for reasons relating to chemistry. To maintain a fire you need heat, fuel and oxygen and it's in the provision of this latter ingredient that crooked logs have the lead over straight ones. Firewood that is packed too densely won't burn well because the process of combustion relies on continuous access to oxygen. Crooked logs build natural air pockets into the fire so that it will maintain its heat and continue to burn smoothly.

By 1694 the phrase had appeared in English writer and wit Thomas D'Urfey's *The comical history of Don Quixote* as 'Crooked logs make good fires,' spelling out even more clearly the benefits of crookedness – though our modern use of 'crooked' as meaning corrupt or criminal doesn't apply.

IT IS ILL PRIZING
OF GREEN BARLEY

As way markers in the agricultural year go, the point at which a farmer's field was a sea of green barley was one to welcome. After all the worries of whether too warm a winter or too changeable a spring might mean they lost their corn to late frosts, there was satisfaction to be had in seeing the crop reach its full height. But as this proverb warns, green barley is only worth anything if it has the chance to ripen.

The saying, which was first recorded in 1721, is one of a number of proverbs popular with those who prefer to err on the side of caution (see also 'Don't count your chickens before they've hatched', p. 78, and 'There's many a slip between cup and lip', p.165) which warn against rejoicing prematurely.

Ripe barley could make a farmer a substantial amount of money if it was of the best quality as it was used in the production of whisky, which was a luxury beyond the pockets of all but the wealthiest of country folk. But a field full of green barley didn't guarantee a good harvest and farmers were still at the mercy of the weather. Thunderstorms that brought heavy rain could lay the barley flat, making it impossible to cut, so barley should only be prized once it had turned the warm golden colour that showed it was fully ripe.

It's the sort of phrase that comes in handy in the modern age for chastising arrogant young upstarts who brag about their business credentials and claim success for enterprises that have yet to prove themselves viable.

WHEN THE MOON LIES ON HER BACK

When the moon lies on her back,
Then the sou'-west wind will crack;
When she rises up and nods,
Then north-easters dry the sod.
If the moon show a silver shield,
Be not afraid to reap your field;
But if she rises haloed round,
Soon will tread on deluged ground.

The moon and her influence over the earth have always loomed large in folklore and there *is* in fact a connection between moon, sun and wind. Since the moon shines by reflecting sunlight, what it looks like to us depends on the angle at which the sun's light hits the moon. The sun's effects on different parts of the earth also cause the wind, which is simply the movement of air from areas of high to low pressure produced by different temperatures. However, these relationships are too complicated to make accurate weather predictions from the shape, or phase, of the moon.

Instead, this ancient rhyme reflects old beliefs based on individual observations passed down the centuries in writings on weather lore (the rhyme appeared in *Symons's Meteorological Magazine* of September 1867), together with more poetic and fanciful notions about both the moon and the weather. *It's sure to be a dry moon if it lies on its back* is a saying from the Welsh borders: the upturned crescent looks as if it can hold water, so the month will be dry. A downturned crescent surely can't hold water, so wet days will follow, although it seems many sailors believe the opposite. Hunters in some parts of the world are said to have stayed at home if they could hang their powderhorns on the upturned crescent of the moon because it's hard to stalk game in a dry forest with footsteps cracking on brittle undergrowth. The haloed moon, though, has a more direct connection with wet weather. The halo is caused by refraction of light by ice crystals in clouds in the earth's atmosphere, so as a warning of a deluge it seems to make good sense.

TALK OF THE DEVIL AND HE WILL APPEAR

When a similar phrase to this one was first used in Ancient Rome it featured a wolf rather than the Devil. Some records of the phrase in Latin call it *'lupus in fabula'* which has given rise to the belief that the saying came from a fable (*fabula*) about a wolf who always appeared when his name was mentioned. But *fabula* can also be translated as 'common talk', and the version used by the Roman comic dramatist Plautus was *'lupus in sermon'* or 'wolf in the conversation', which suggests that it may simply have originated as an expression with the same meaning as our own version.

In England the Devil appeared in the proverb from around the sixteenth century, when belief in his cunning wiles meant that the phrase was taken literally as a warning against uttering his name.

Nowadays we use the first part of the phrase – 'talk of the Devil' in those uncanny instances where a person unexpectedly enters the room when their name is hot on our lips. Often it's delivered jovially to the person themselves and is simply a way of expressing surprise at their arrival. Sometimes, though, when we're talking about someone we don't think so highly of, a little of the old association with the Devil lingers in our meaning as we whisper the phrase.

ONION SKINS
VERY THIN

Onion skins very thin
Mild winter coming in;
Onion skins thick and tough
Coming winter cold and rough.

This is one of many traditional folklore verses which attempt to predict long-range weather conditions. In a similar way, according to the *Dictionary of Plant Lore* by Donald Watts, the thickness of hazelnut shells is said to be an indication of the weather to come. Thicker shells predict harder winters, as though the hazelnut had on its winter coat.

Another useful indicator to rural dwellers who would have lived close to woodland are acorns. All over Europe a large crop of acorns is said to presage a severe winter. Other plant predictors are less ambitious (and perhaps more reliable) in their range. 'A blackthorn winter' describes the period of cold weather in springtime that often follows warm March days which bring the blackthorn (sloe; *Prunus spinosa*) into early flower. It may be tempting to think that traditional predictions such as onion skin thickness have stood the test of time only because they rely on selective memory: people remember when they predict correctly and forget when they're wrong. However, increasing scientific understanding of long-term weather patterns (drought cycles, the El Niño/La Niña-Southern Oscillation, and other global climate systems in which variations in ocean temperature produce consistent weather changes in the year ahead) may add some credence to ancient folklore wisdom. Plant and animal populations can be sensitive to subtle meteorological and climatic conditions that go unnoticed by human observers, until their subsequent, more obvious effects are manifest. These kinds of biological indicators may be responsible for some of the truths preserved through long centuries of observation and experience.

KILL NOT THE GOOSE THAT LAYS THE GOLDEN EGGS

This sage piece of advice comes from Æsop's fable about a farmer who loses everything through greed. In the story the farmer realizes that his goose is laying golden eggs. One golden egg a day for the foreseeable future would have meant the farmer would never want for anything again, but the farmer wanted instant access to the gold, which he believed must be stored up inside the goose, so he killed the goose only to find that there was no store of gold, and with the goose dead, there would be no more golden eggs.

It's a tale that is popular with children, who empathize with the farmer's puzzlement that the goose's insides aren't full of gold but simultaneously enjoy occupying the moral high ground because they would never have killed the goose to try to get at it. Sadly, the moral lesson often seems to fade with age and most of us are guilty of at least day-dreaming about ways in which we might get rich quick. Interestingly, though, this isn't a straightforward 'greed is wrong' morality tale, since what it teaches is how to preserve the slow but steady acquisition of wealth.

We still use the phrase today as a warning against making rash decisions that endanger our livelihoods, and also use the term 'goose that laid the golden egg' to describe business schemes that seem to be guaranteed money-spinners.

ENOUGH IS AS GOOD AS A FEAST

This saying advocating moderation in all things appeared for the first time in print in 1470 in William Caxton's publication of Sir Thomas Malory's *Le Morte d'Arthur*:

Inowghe is as good as a feste.

In his introduction Caxton instructed readers to use the tales as a source of moral guidance, saying: 'Doo after the good and leve the evyl, and it shal brynge you to good fame and renommee.' The legends of King Arthur captured the medieval imagination and stories of the Knights of the Round Table were read aloud and passed on through word of mouth so their influence spread far beyond the literate population.

It was clearly well established by the time Heywood published his *Dialogue of Proverbs* in 1546:

> *For folke say, enough is as good as a feast.*

This particular proverb must have appealed to those for whom a feast was beyond the realms of possibility and who probably took from it some reassurance that having enough to eat was more important than having a surplus. But the phrase was applied to other matters, too.

Sir Walter Scott showed how it might be used to quell a young man's appetite for battle by using it in his celebrated novel *Waverley* in 1814:

> *'... If you saw war on the grand scale – sixty or a hundred thousand men in the field on each side!'*
> *'I am not at all curious, Colonel – Enough, says our homely proverb, is as good as a feast.'*

The phrase is still used today, metaphorically and literally – as at the dinner table when we've had enough to eat or when showing restraint by declining the offer of seconds. In fact, in the modern age with obesity levels rising unstoppably, enough might in fact be said to be infinitely better than a feast.

A DRIPPING JUNE
SETS ALL IN TUNE

Most proverbs from weather lore seem to suggest that an ideal farming year would see a long, cold winter, a bright, wet spring, a warm, clear summer and a mild autumn that stays dry until the last of the harvesting is over. Within that general picture, though, are certain subtleties that it's hard to keep track of unless you're a farmer. This phrase was first recorded in *The Agreeable Companion*, an anthology of 'wit and good humour' published in 1792, and is a shortened version of the full saying: 'A dry May and a dripping June bringeth all things into tune.' In many ways it's self-explanatory: rainy weather in the month of June gives corn crops, fruit trees and flowers the final watering they need to ripen or bloom over the summer.

But the saying may also have referred to the influence of a wet June on the rest of the months in the year.

While long-range weather forecasting was impossible before satellite technology, country people did believe, probably as a result of observing that things happened this way for enough years in a row to make it a rule, that if June was wet, August and September would be dry. Late summer and early autumn is harvest time and the most important time of year for the rain to stay away. Like many sayings relating to the timing of rainfall there is an unspoken element of superstition in the phrase. If you noted the rain in June and welcomed it as a sign that everything was being set in tune, it might influence fate to make it so.

ALL CATS ARE GREY IN THE DARK

As the associates of witches, cats appear often in folklore and those to whom magical powers were attached were usually black. Black was the colour of the Devil and had been associated with mourning and death since the times of the Ancient Greeks; it was also the colour of animals that were really demons or witches who had taken animal form and a black cat crossing your path was said to be unlucky – or sometimes said to be lucky. In darkness, though, as this proverb advocating equality points out, all cats look grey, which meant that black cats were treated no differently from cats of any other colour.

The phrase first appeared in the 1549 edition of John Heywood's *Dialogue of Proverbs*:

> ### *When all candels be out, all cats be grey. All thyngs are then of one colour.*

Thomas Fuller collected it in his *Gnomologia* (1732) as:

> ### *All Cats are alike grey in the Night.*

The American statesman Benjamin Franklin put it to extraordinary use in a letter written in 1745 in which he explained the advantages of having an older woman as a lover. 'And as in the dark all Cats are grey,' he wrote, 'the Pleasure of corporal Enjoyment with an old Woman is at least equal, and frequently superior.'

We still use the phrase to explain why we're not being particularly discerning about something, either because we've got no way of telling the options apart or because we don't really mind which option we pick. We sometimes use the version 'All cats are grey after midnight' as an alternative to blaming an unlikely conquest on 'beer goggles' if we're putting the phrase to Franklin's use.

IF FEBRUARY GIVES MUCH SNOW

If February gives much snow,
A fine summer it doth foreshow.

Ever hopeful of better times to come, rural weather watchers took the arrival of snowy conditions in February as a sign not so much that the summer would be warm and dry, but that it would be productive. In fact, this month was the subject of several pieces of weather lore. *A handbook of weather folk-lore; being a collection of proverbial sayings in various languages relating to the weather, with explanatory and illustrative notes,* published in 1873, lists one from Wales that bears testament to the strength of feeling evoked by the month's climate:

The Welshman had rather see his dam
on the bier Than see a fair Februeer.

Meaning that he'd rather see his mother dead than endure a fine February. An English proverb from the same publication says:

When gnats dance in February, the
husbandman becomes a beggar.

Gnats breed best in warm, humid temperatures so this is further evidence of the disastrous consequences of mild weather early in the year for farmers, whose harvests could be ruined if crops came out too soon and were later killed by frost.

Plenty of snow in February was infinitely preferable, keeping everything dormant and safely in the ground until spring. According to weather lore it also has a stabilizing impact on temperatures in other months, setting the tone for a year in which the weather would be appropriate to the season and thus produce a bumper harvest come autumn.

Other, briefer versions of the saying exist: 'Frost year fruit year', 'Year of snow, fruit will grow' and 'A snow year, a rich year'.

As proverbs, any of these phrases might be used in an effort to encourage someone through a time of hardship by reminding them that a period that has its share of metaphorical snow is likely to turn out to be a good one once the difficult time has passed. (See also 'Better a wolf in the fold, than a fine February', p.22.)

Thanks to John Rhodes, Lorna Rhodes, Teddy Howe, Heather Rhodes, Annette Hibberd and Matt Hibberd, and to Toby Buchan and the editorial and design team at Michael O'Mara Books, especially Ana Bježančević, Dominique Enright and Andy Armitage.

BIBLIOGRAPHY

All biblical quotations are from the King James Bible (Authorized Version)

Apperson, G. L., *The Wordsworth Dictionary of Proverbs*, Wordsworth Editions 1993 and 2006

Brewer, Ebenezer Cobham, *Dictionary of Phrase and Fable*, Wordsworth Editions 2001

Buchanan, Daniel Crump, *Japanese Proverbs and Sayings*, University of Oklahoma Press 1965

Cooper, Ernest R., *Mardles from Suffolk: A Taste of East Anglian Humour*, Countryside Books 1989

Currie, Ian, *Red Sky at Night: Weather Sayings for All Seasons*, Frosted Earth 1992

Flavell, Linda and Roger, *Dictionary of Proverbs and their Origins*, Kyle Cathie Ltd 1994

Flexner, Stuart and Doris, *Wise Words and Wives' Tales: The Origins, Meanings and Time-Honored Wisdom of Proverbs and Folk Sayings Olde and New*, Avon Books 1993

Parkinson, Judy, *Spilling the Beans on the Cat's Pyjamas: Popular Expressions – What They Mean and Where We Got Them*, Michael O'Mara Books 2009

Partington, Charles Frederick, *The British Cyclopaedia of Biography: containing the lives of distinguished men of all ages and countries, with portraits, residences, autographs, and monuments*, Volume 2 (Google eBook)

Ratcliffe, Susan (ed.), *The Oxford Dictionary of Phrase, Saying and Quotation*, Oxford University Press 2006

Shapiro, Fred R., *The Yale Book of Quotations*, Yale University Press 2006

Simpson, John and Speake, Jennifer, *The Concise Oxford Dictionary of Proverbs* , Oxford University Press 2003

Sommer, Robin Langley, *Nota Bene: A Guide to Familiar Latin Quotes and Phrases*, Past Times 1996

Taggart, Caroline, *An Apple a Day: Old-fashioned proverbs and why they still work*, Michael O'Mara Books 2009

Taylor, James W., *Reminiscences of a Fenman*, privately published, 1980

Thiselton Dyer, T. F., *The Folk-Lore of Plants*, first published 1888, The Echo Library 2008

Titelman, Gregory Y., *The Random House Dictionary of Popular Proverbs and Sayings*, Random House 1996

Watts, Donald, *Dictionary of Plant Lore*, Academic Press 2007

www.answers.com
www.archive.org

www.englishproverbs.org
www.famousquotessite.com
www.oed.com
www.phrases.org.uk
www.poetryintranslation.com
www.uwsp.edu
www.word-origins.com

Maxims and proverbs have been collected enthusiastically over the centuries. The sixteenth to eighteenth centuries are particularly rich in compilations of proverbs, epigrams, homilies or even unusual words, many of them running to several revised and enlarged editions. Those I refer to most frequently are:

John Heywood (*c.*1497–*c.* 1580): *A dialogue conteinyng the nomber in effect of all the prouerbes in the Englishe tongue* (shortened to *A Dialogue of Proverbs*), 1546; *Epigrammes*, 1555

John Clarke (d.1658): *Parœmiologia Anglo-Latina*, 1639

James Howell (1594–1666): *Paramoigraphy* (Proverbs), 1659

John Ray (1627–1705): *Collection of English Proverbs,* 1670; *Collection of Proverbs,* 1678

Thomas Fuller (1654–1734): *Gnomologia: Adagies and Proverbs, Wise Sentences and Witty Sayings,* 1732 (not to be confused with the churchman and historian Thomas Fuller, 1608–61, also cited in this book).

INDEX